LOST DUNDEE

BRIAN KING

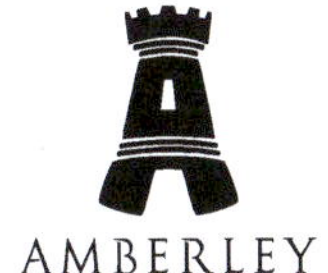

AMBERLEY

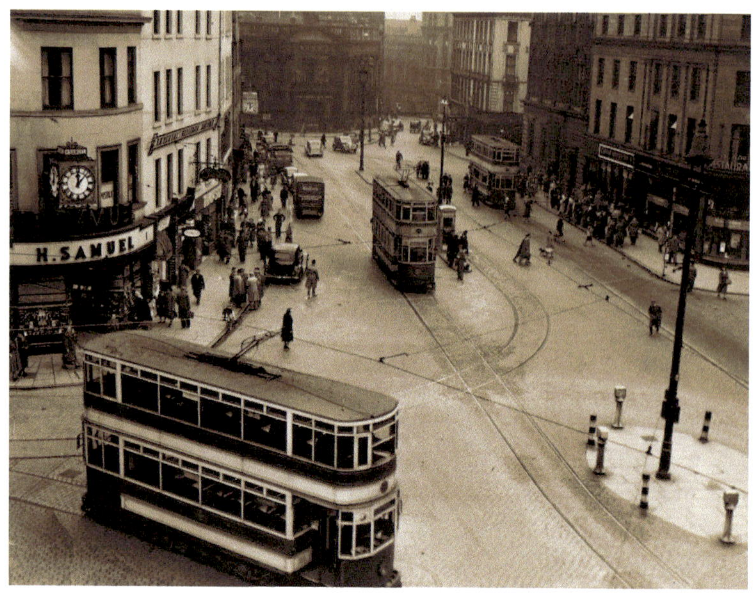

This edition first published 2025

Amberley Publishing
The Hill, Stroud
Gloucestershire GL5 4EP

www.amberley-books.com

Copyright © Brian King, 2025

The right of Brian King to be identified as the Author
of this work has been asserted in accordance with the
Copyrights, Designs and Patents Act 1988.

All rights reserved. No part of this book may be reprinted
or reproduced or utilised in any form or by any electronic,
mechanical or other means, now known or hereafter invented, including
photocopying and recording, or in any information
storage or retrieval system, without the permission in writing
from the Publishers.

British Library Cataloguing in Publication Data.
A catalogue record for this book is available from the British Library.

ISBN 978 1 3981 2157 7 (print)
ISBN 978 1 3981 2158 4 (ebook)

Typeset by Simon and Sons ITES Services Pvt. Ltd., Chennai, India.
Printed in Great Britain.

Appointed GPSR EU Representative: Easy Access System Europe Oü, 16879218
Address: Mustamäe tee 50, 10621, Tallinn, Estonia
Contact Details: gpsr.requests@easproject.com, +358 40 500 3575

Contents

Introduction

There is a plaque on the City Chambers in Dundee commemorating its predecessor, the Town House, which once stood nearby. There is a commemorative stone in the City Square that marks where the Town House once stood. Across the road is a clock attached to the side of a building in the High Street which has a model of the Town House on top. There is another model of it outside the Pillars public house, which itself takes its name from the building's colonnade. Almost a century after it was demolished, it seems that Dundee still fondly remembers the building that was its focal point for two centuries. Any regret that the city had about the destruction of the Town House in 1932, though, was not reflected in the move towards conservation in the remainder of the twentieth century. Instead, a time of unparalleled change in the city saw many more demolitions.

As time passes, the loss of buildings is inevitable in any town or city but Dundee also suffered from a loss of whole streets, which were swept away in the second half of the twentieth century to make way for contemporary shopping developments and increased motor traffic. Chief among these was the Overgate, one of Dundee's main thoroughfares with a history stretching back to the early days of the burgh when it was known as Argyllgait. While many of its buildings were in a dilapidated state by the beginning of the 1960s, the street was denied the chance to evolve while retaining its character and was entirely replaced with a modern shopping centre and hotel. This also caused an interruption in what had been the seamless progression from the city centre to the West Port and the Hawkhill beyond. The Overgate now came to an abrupt end at a busy main road which also served to slice another old Dundee street, the Nethergate, into two distinct sections. At the other side of the city centre, the replacement of the Wellgate with the shopping centre of the same name broke the continuous incline leading to the Hilltown and the north of the city. In the 1960s Dundee also lost its direct connection to the River Tay when the main city centre docks were filled in to make way for the landfall of the Tay Road Bridge and its approach roads.

In the late twentieth and early twenty-first century attempts to make up for the perceived failures of the past meant that the Dundee that emerged in the 1960s and 1970s itself began to disappear. In particular, the Overgate and waterfront areas were redeveloped once again. Buildings such as the Overgate shopping centre, Tayside House and the Angus Hotel were demolished. Many people in Dundee saw the same buildings rise and fall in the course of their lifetimes in a way that did not happen in previous generations.

It is not only the physical city that has changed in the period covered by this book. The world of work in Dundee has changed considerably over the years. As happened throughout the country, traditional manufacturing jobs declined in the second half of the twentieth century. In Dundee's case this meant the jute industry in particular. Indeed, only the third of the traditional three Js – jute, jam and journalism – that the city was once known for continues to flourish today.

If the working lives of Dundonians have changed, so too has the way that they spend their leisure time. While many activities shown in this book still take place, changes in society and in technology mean that many of the ways that we spend our spare time are much more tailored to the individual and less of a communal experience than they once were.

Our journey in search of lost Dundee also looks at the means of transport we used to travel about the city. Not only have the vehicles changed over the decades but they have, in turn, changed the face of Dundee. Roads were constructed or improved to accommodate trams and motor transport. The construction of the railway bridge connected the city to the south in a new way by cutting journey times. The Tay Road Bridge did the same for motor traffic but also ended the centuries-old ferry service.

This book takes us back to a Dundee that is gone. Even where aspects of the physical city of the past still exist, time has changed their appearance. Things continue to change, of course, and present-day Dundee will one day fade into history. We live in a time, though, when most people routinely carry equipment capable of recording their environment. This book owes a debt to those who, at a time when it was more difficult, recorded what is now lost Dundee.

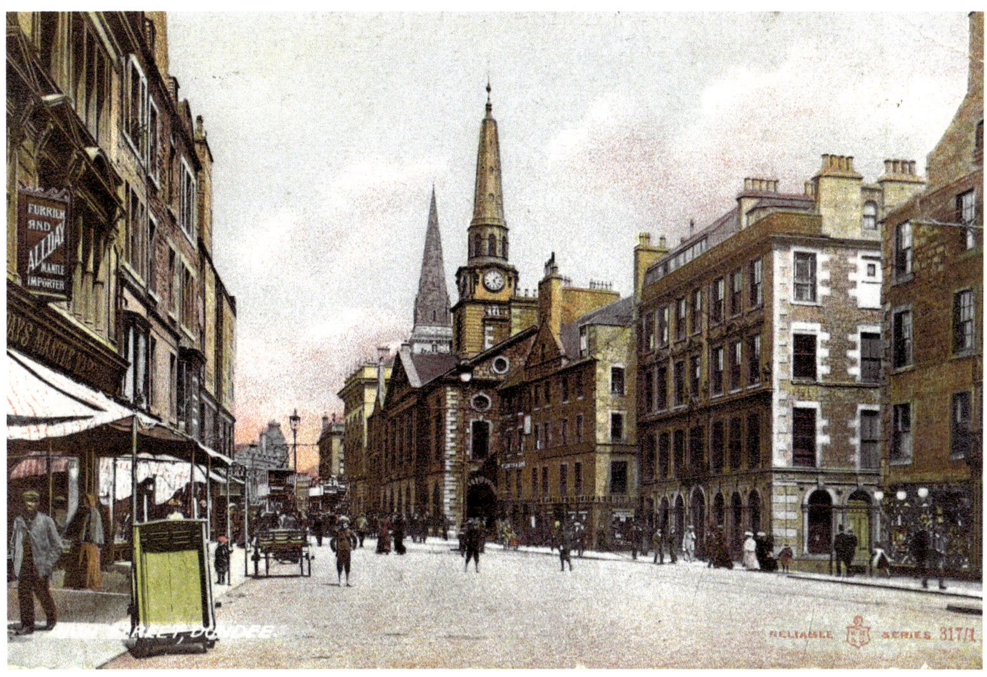

Lost Buildings

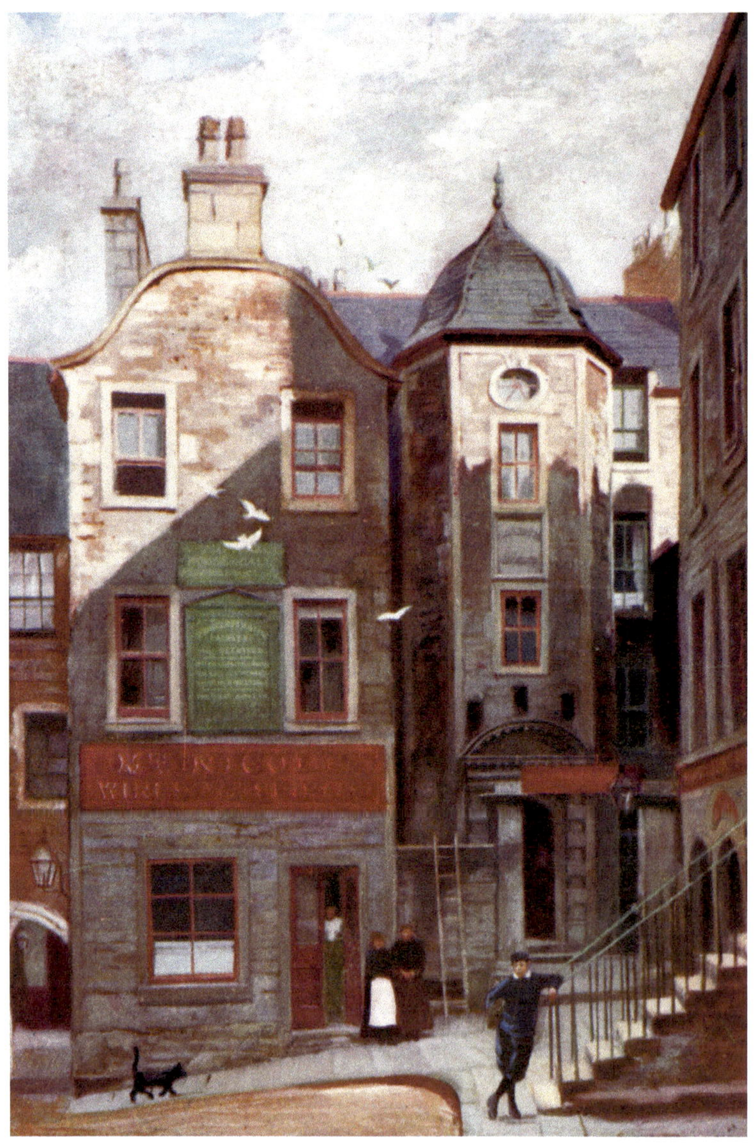

Strathmartine's Lodging, The Vault.

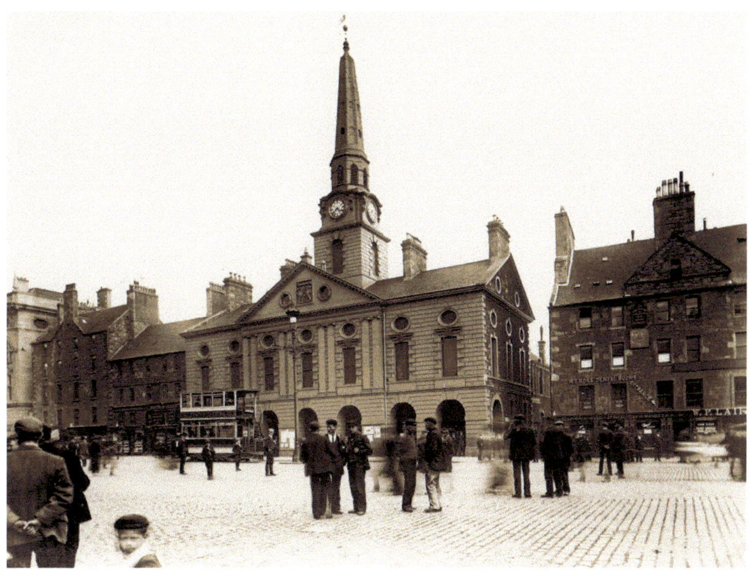

Town House

Dundee's Town House was built in the 1730s to a design by William Adam, father of Robert and James Adam, the influential eighteenth-century architects and designers. It replaced an earlier tollbooth on the same site. The council and guildry chambers were on the first floor and the town's jail was on the floor above. Known locally as 'the Pillars', the colonnade of the Town House was a popular meeting place and contained several shops including the original Braithwaite's coffee shop.

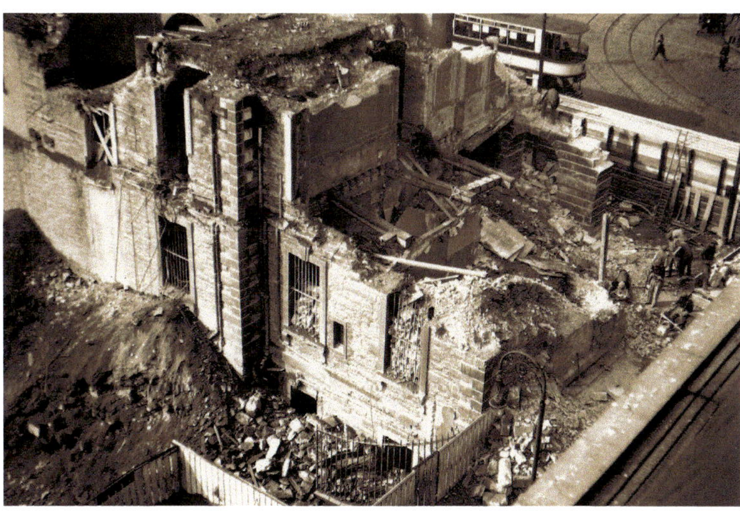

Demolition of the Town House

Many were unhappy with the decision to demolish the Town House to make way for the City Square. Proposals were made for its rebuilding elsewhere and, when demolition began, the stones were numbered in case this took place. In the end, though, the building was completely demolished as this 1932 photograph shows. It was, perhaps, Dundee's first major architectural loss of the twentieth century but, as we will see, it would not be the last.

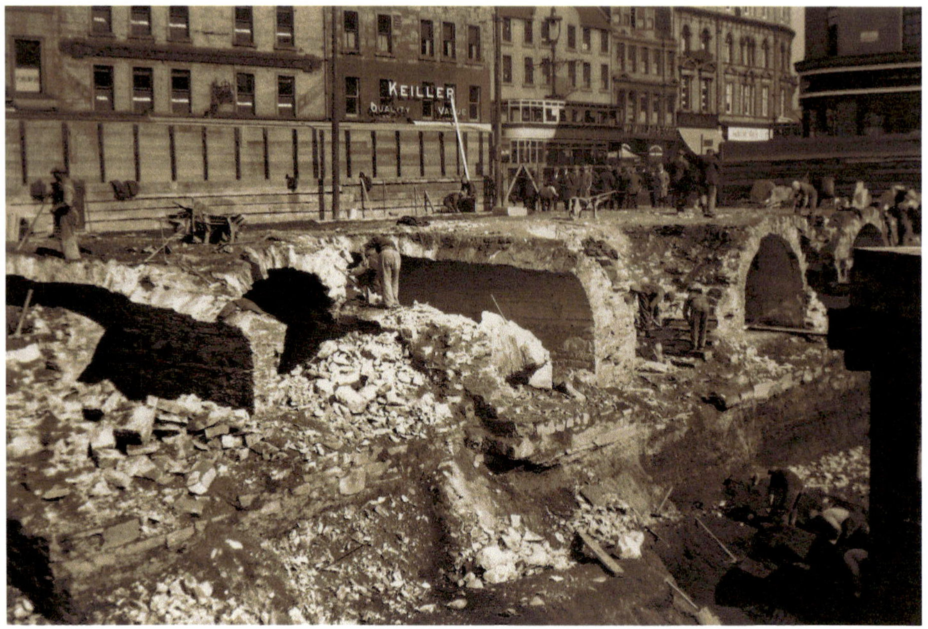

Vaults Below the Town House

It seems that every trace of the Town House was removed to make way for the City Square. Here the workmen are seen destroying the vaulted cellars below street level. One of these was at one time used as a prison cell gaining the nickname 'the thief's hole'. Among its more unusual occupants was a tree which had been planted by local residents as a 'Tree of Liberty' in 1792, but was temporarily removed to the cell by the local authorities.

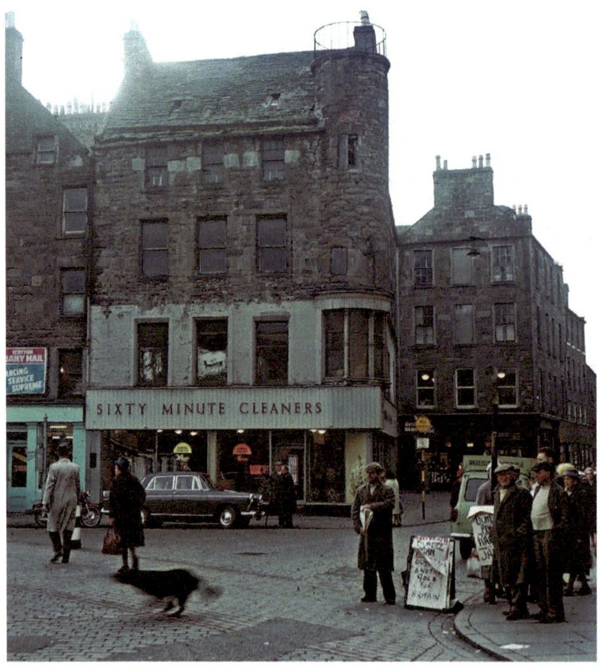

General Monck's Headquarters

If you look closely at this picture, you will see that there is a metal plaque on the left-hand side of the Sixty Minute Cleaners. The plaque stated that the building was both the birthplace of Anna, Duchess of Monmouth, and Headquarters of General Monck during the Siege of Dundee 1651. This image dates from the early 1960s shortly before it was demolished to make way for the first Overgate shopping centre and is now the site of a Primark store.

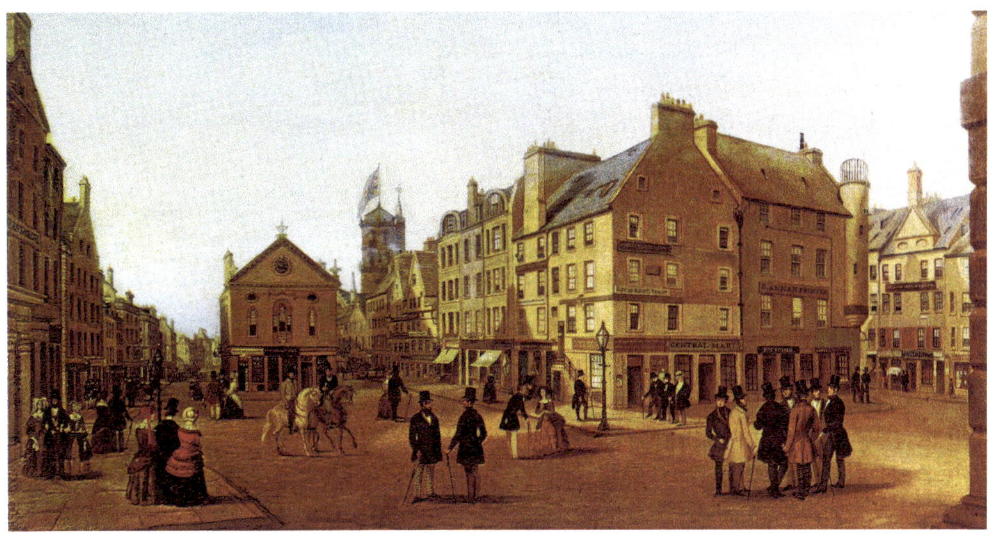

Union Hall

This nineteenth-century painting by George McGillivary shows the Union Hall, which dated from the 1780s. It was originally a place of worship housing an Episcopal congregation and was known as the English Chapel. Like the Trades Hall, the corresponding landmark building at the other end of the High Street, it was designed by the Burgh Architect Samuel Bell. Following the departure of the chapel's congregation, the building was used for public meetings. The Union Hall was demolished in 1876.

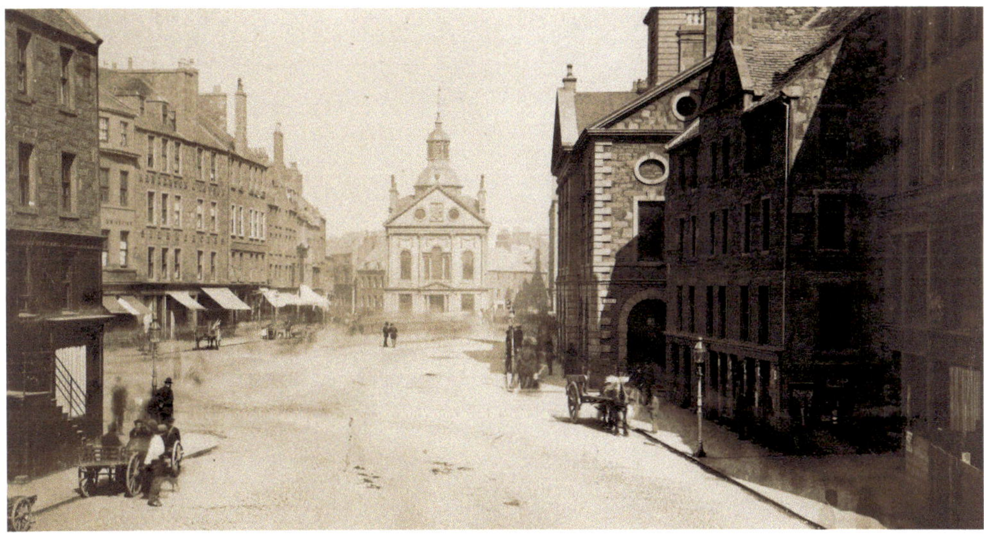

Trades Hall

Dominating the east end of Dundee's High Street, on a site that had once been the town's shambles (or open-air slaughterhouse), the Trades Hall was built in 1776 to a design by Samuel Bell, as we have seen. It was home to the Nine Incorporated Trades of Dundee – the associations of Baxters (bakers), Cordiners (shoemakers), Skinners (glovers), Tailors, Bonnetmakers, Fleshers (butchers), Hammermen (metalworkers), Weavers and Dyers. Prior to this, their meeting place had been the Howff graveyard. It was demolished in 1878.

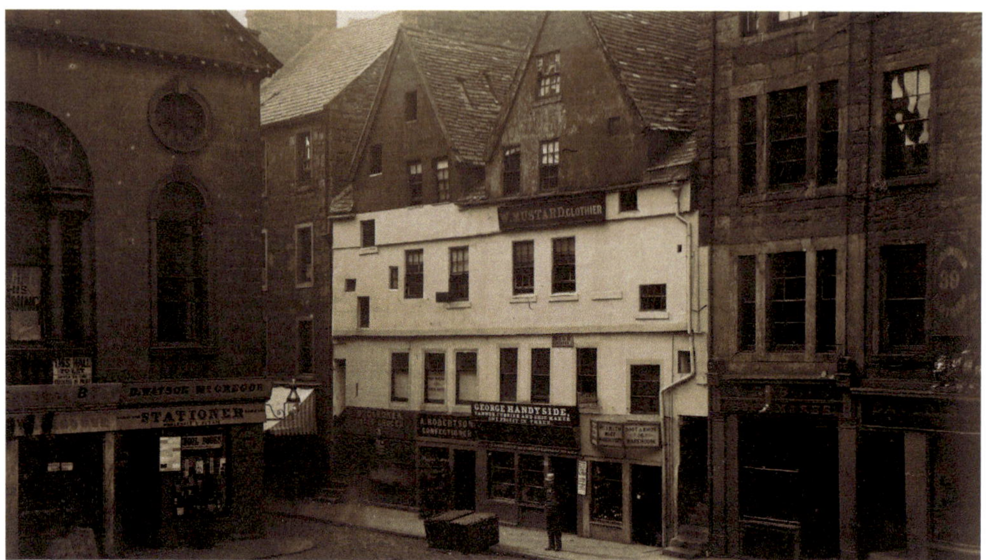

Our Lady Warkstairs

Situated opposite the top of Crichton Street, Our Lady Warkstairs was a timber-fronted building, said to be the last in Dundee. Originally built before 1500, it was believed to have once been an almshouse associated with the Church of St Mary. It was rebuilt around 1550 after having being burnt down during the English occupation in the 1540s. During its demolition in 1879, the pillars that supported the projecting façade before the creation of process the ground floor shops were rediscovered.

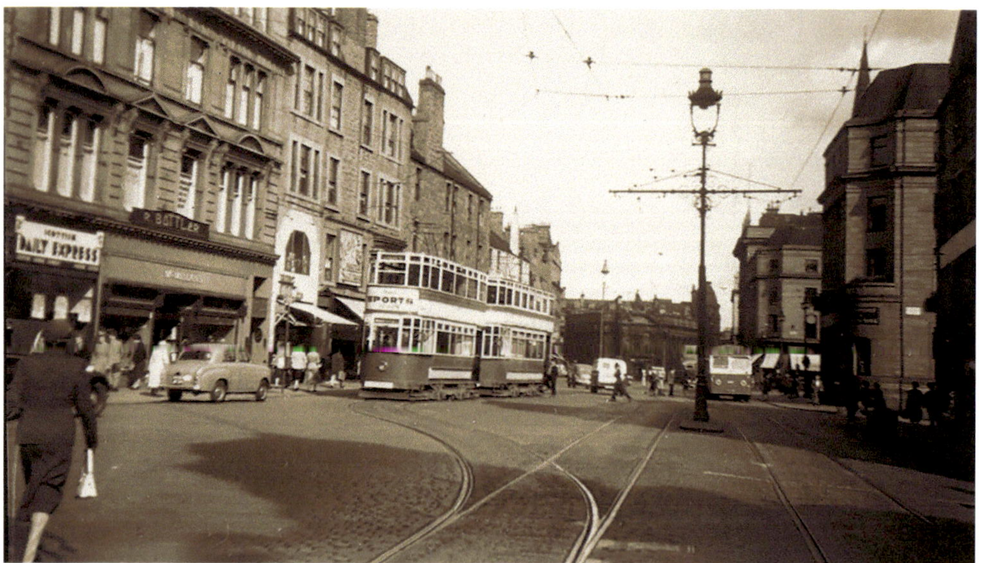

High Street

The site of Our Lady Warkstairs is visible on the left-hand side of this image. All the buildings on this side of the street were demolished in the 1960s and to make way for what is now the Primark store. The buildings on the other side of the road and the view straight ahead remain largely unchanged to this day.

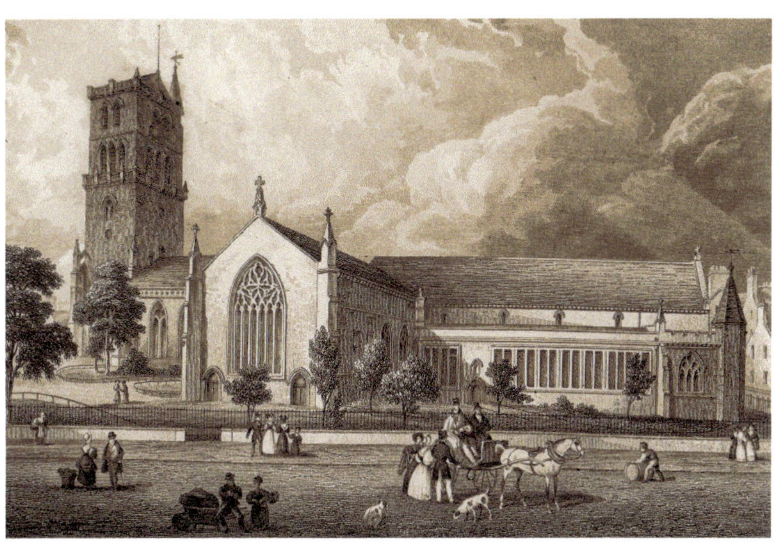

City Churches

The church of St Mary the Virgin was founded around 1190 by David, Earl of Huntingdon. The building suffered badly in the various invasions of Dundee and the church was destroyed and rebuilt several times. As it was rebuilt, it became home to four separate congregations. In January 1841, a devastating fire broke out that soon engulfed the churches. Most of the structure was subsequently demolished and rebuilt. This illustration shows the churches as they appeared before the fire.

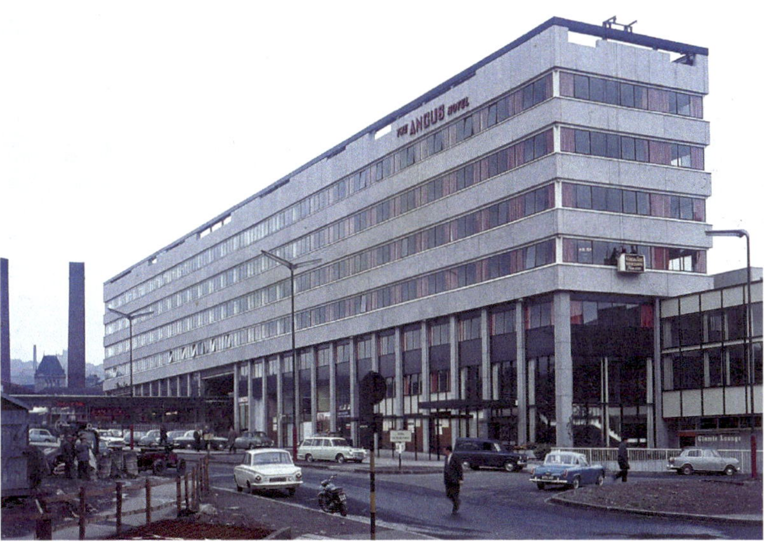

The Angus Hotel

The Angus Hotel opened in 1964 and this photograph dates from around that time. It had been built as part of the Overgate redevelopment at a cost of £450,000, with a further £52,000 being spent on high-quality furnishings. Celebrity visitors included David Bowie, Billy Connolly, Freddie Mercury and Rod Stewart. The brutalist style which had appeared so modern in the 1960s soon became outdated, though, and it was demolished as part of the next Overgate redevelopment.

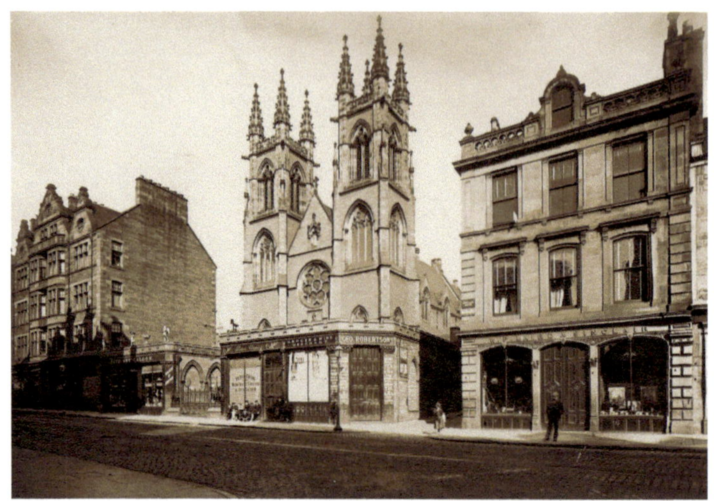

St Enoch's Church, Nethergate

St Enoch's Free Church congregation was worshipping at premises at Long Wynd when the ground at nearby Nethergate was acquired in 1866. The church, with its two 100-foot-high towers, was opened in 1874. Similar to St Paul's Church, which survives on the other side of the Nethergate, St Enoch's had a single-storey shop on either side of the entrance. The buildings to the right of this picture were demolished to make way for the inner ring road.

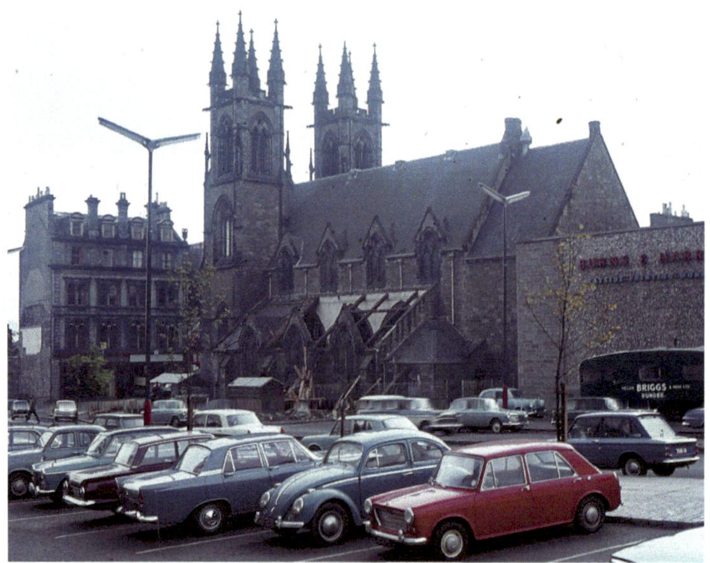

Demolition of St Enoch's

This 1964 view, taken from the car park of the Angus Hotel, shows the beginning of the process of demolition of St Enoch's, which in its latter years was a Church of Scotland. The only remnant that survives today is the western shop. The building that was eventually built on the site – originally a Bank of Scotland but now the offices of Gilson Gray solicitors – when viewed from the Nethergate offers a vague reflection of St Enoch's twin towers.

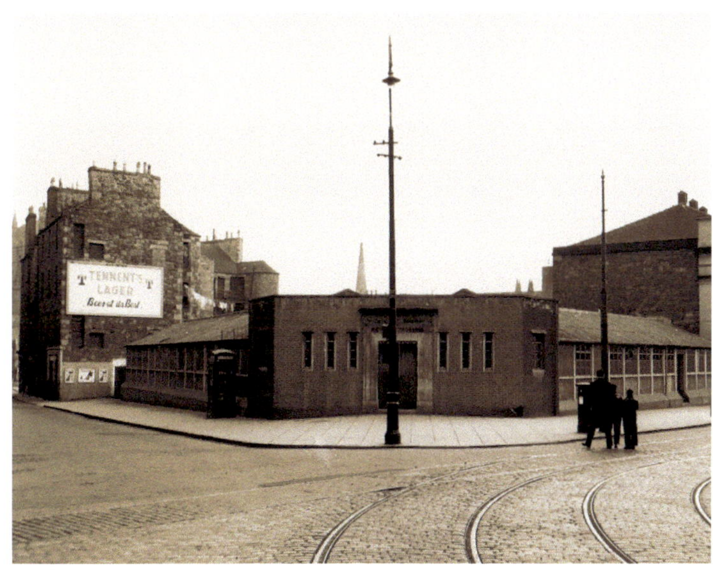

Junction of Overgate and South Tay Street

Unlike its northern counterpart South Tay Street still survives today. It is shown here at its junction with the Overgate. Most of the buildings in this view were demolished in the 1960s but the position of the Old Steeple and the spire of St Paul's in the Nethergate help to identify the location. The Cinerama glimpsed on the right of the picture was a former church and, in 1929, became the first place to show 'talking pictures' in Dundee.

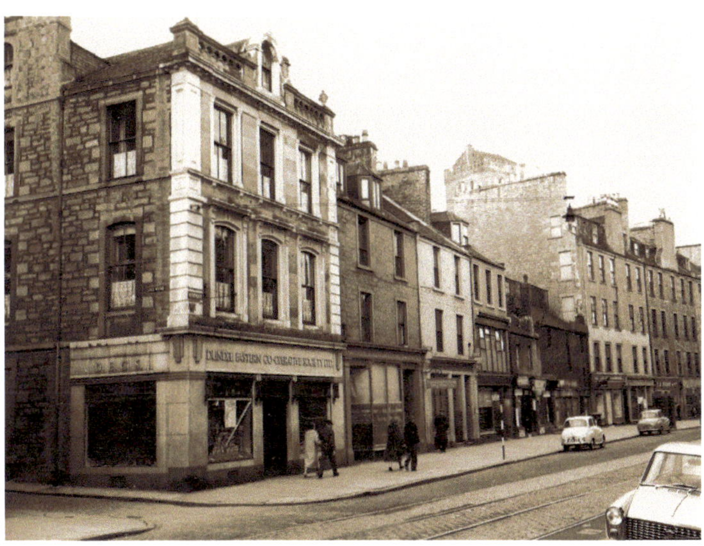

Nethergate

The Old Steeple is the only surviving building in this photograph. This part of the Nethergate was demolished to make way for the inner ring road, which effectively split the street into two sections. On the left-hand side of the photograph is the entrance to Long Wynd, which ran roughly parallel to South Tay Street and met the Overgate as it made its way towards the West Port.

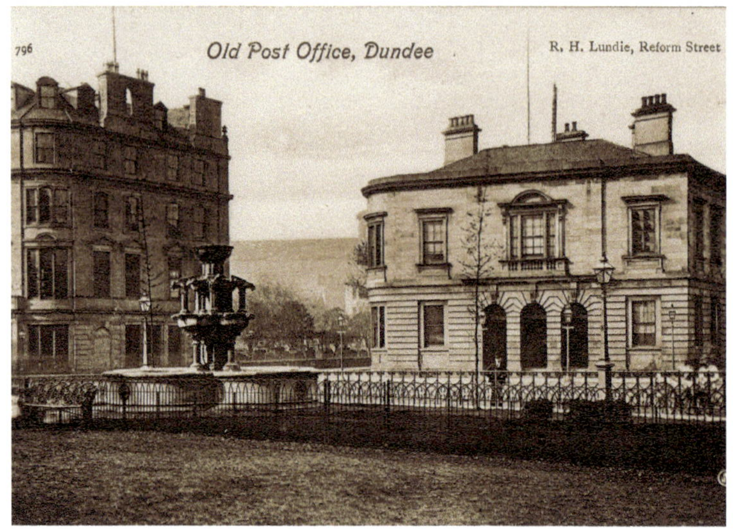

General Post Office

This post office building opened in 1862 on the site of what is now DC Thomson's Courier Building. It was Dundee's main post office until 1898 when a new, more elaborate, GPO building opened in Meadowside to a design by the Office of Works architect Walter Wood Robertson, who was also responsible for designing or adapting many of the main post offices in Scotland's other towns and cities. The Courier Building opened in 1906.

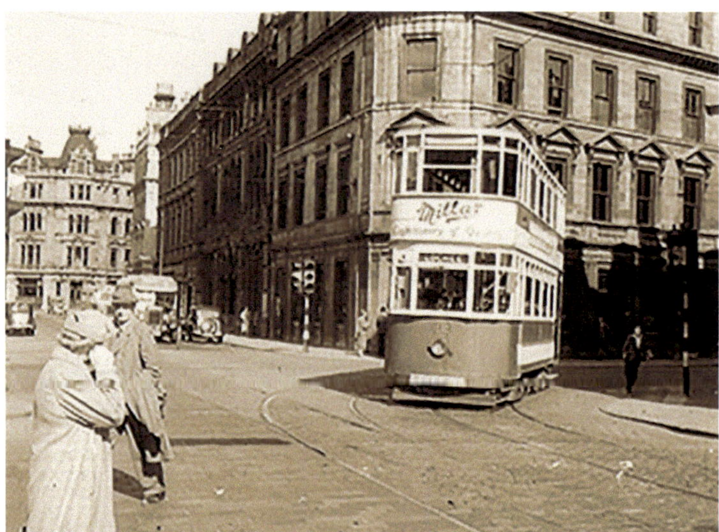

The Eastern Club

The elaborately designed building visible to the left of the tram at Albert Square was built to house the Eastern Club, a gentlemen's club whose members were drawn from the local elites. It was formally opened in October 1870 with a dinner attended by the Earl of Dalhousie. The building survived well into the twentieth century as this picture shows. Sadly, it was demolished in the 1960s to make way for a modern bank building.

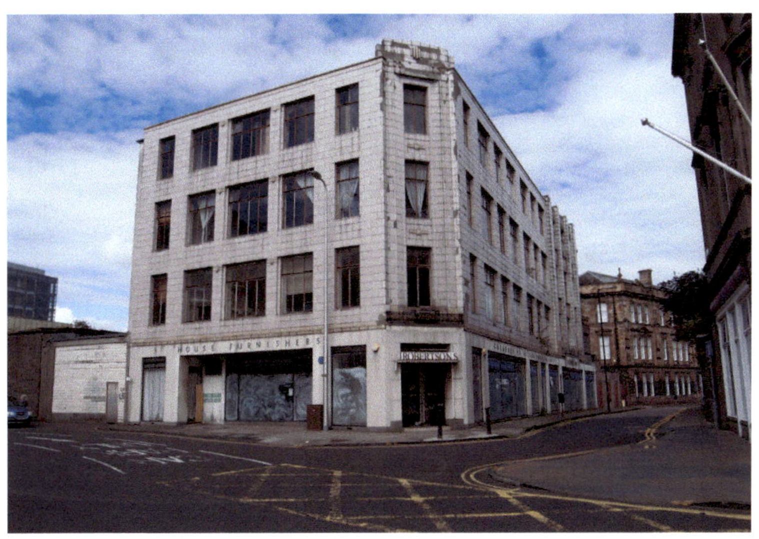

Willison House

Orcadian John Robertson originally set up as a furniture manufacturer in the Cowgate in the late nineteenth century. Remaining in the family, the business moved to Barrack Street in 1929 and this striking art deco building – Willison House – with its eighteen display windows was completed in 1935. The business closed in 2011. It was hoped that the building could be converted to other use but a devastating fire in 2022 left it in a dangerous condition and it was demolished.

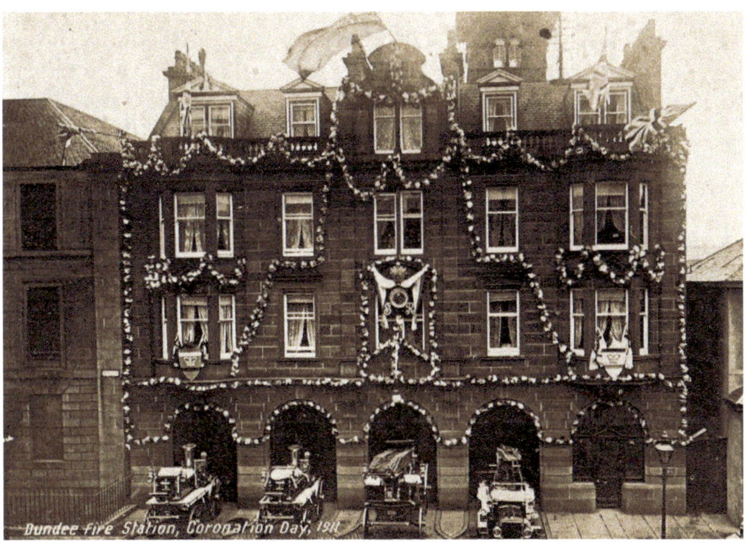

Central Fire Station

This photograph shows the Central Fire Station in West Bell Street decked out for the coronation of George V in 1911. It had opened in 1900. There was accommodation for the Fire Master and his deputy on the first floor and for eight firemen on the floors above. Originally, there were also stables as the fire appliances were horse-drawn. In May 1970 a new Central Fire Station was opened at Blackness Road and the West Bell Street premises was later demolished.

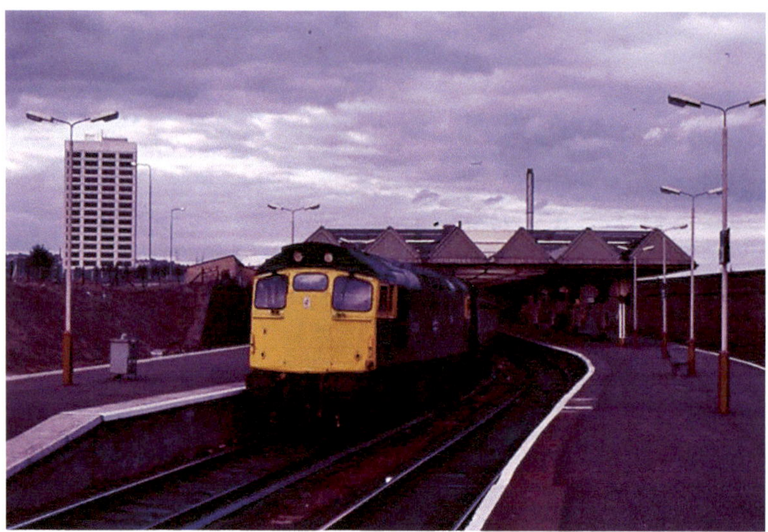

Tayside House

For around forty years, one of the first buildings that a visitor to Dundee city centre would see was the sixteen-storey tower Tayside House, shown here from the railway station. It was built to house the offices of Tayside Regional Council, which had come into being by local government reorganisation in 1974 and lasted until the next reorganisation in 1996. Never particularly popular, Tayside House was a predictable casualty of plans to redevelop the area.

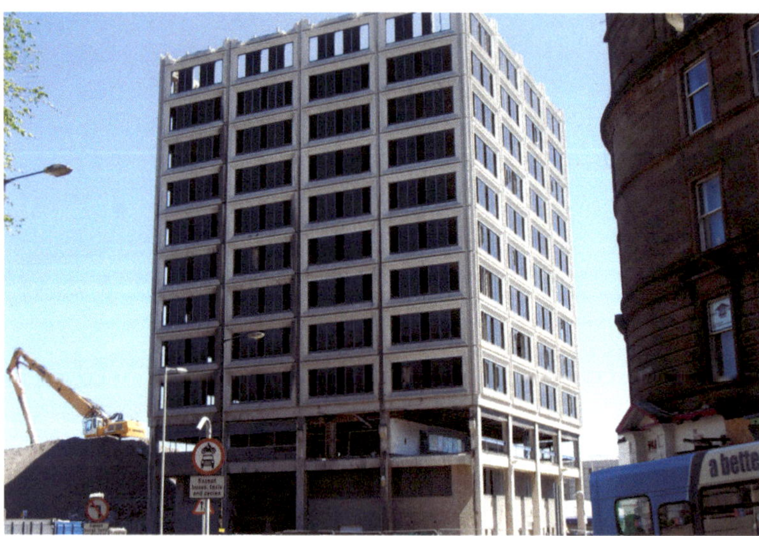

Demolition of Tayside House

This picture was taken in August 2013 during the demolition of Tayside House as part of the waterfront redevelopment. Unlike various high-rise blocks across the city (known in Dundee as multis), the building could not be blown up. This was because it was feared that any such explosion would damage the Dock Street railway tunnel which runs underground nearby. Instead, it was taken down gradually.

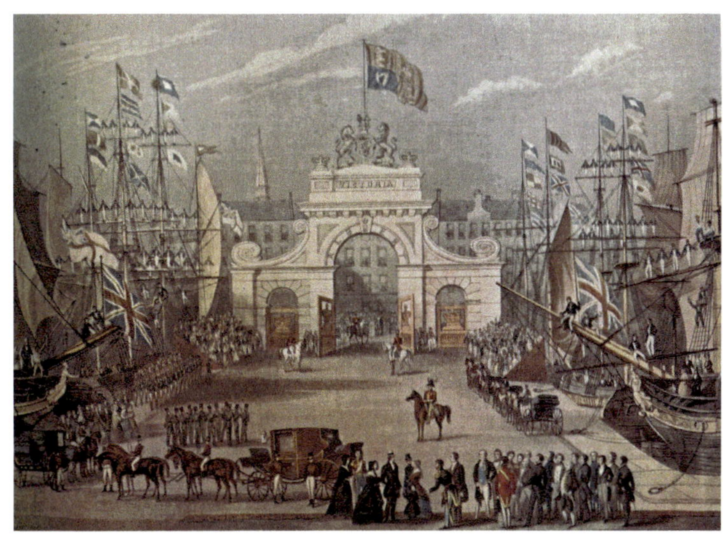

Original Royal Arch

Queen Victoria visited Dundee twice during her long reign. The first time was in 1844 when she and her husband Prince Albert arrived at Dundee's docks. This temporary decorative arch was erected there to mark the occasion. Her second visit was as a widow on Friday 20 June 1879 when her train crossed the ill-fated original Tay Bridge. She wrote in her diary, 'It took us, I should say, about eight minutes going over. The view was very fine.'

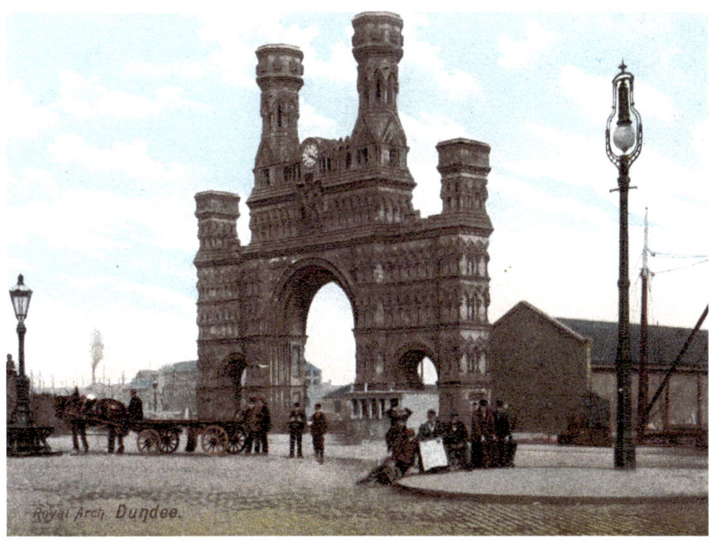

Royal Arch

A few years after the Queen's original visit, a more permanent stone structure was put in place, designed by the Edinburgh-born architect John Thomas Rochead, who would later design the Wallace Monument near Stirling. Like all such triumphal arches, it was designed to be commemorative rather than fulfil any practical purpose. Nevertheless, it did become a well-known local landmark.

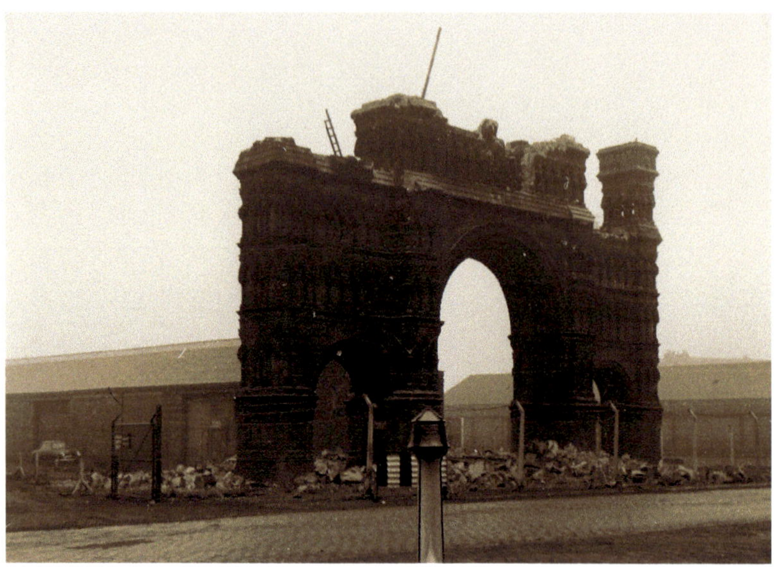

Demolition of the Royal Arch

The Royal Arch stood for more than a hundred years. Like the docks whose entrance it marked, though, it was a casualty of the redevelopment associated with the construction of the Tay Road Bridge. Despite objections, it was demolished in 1964 and the rubble thrown into the King William IV and the Earl Grey Docks. The arch's foundations were rediscovered during the twenty-first century redevelopment of the area and its site is now marked by granite slabs.

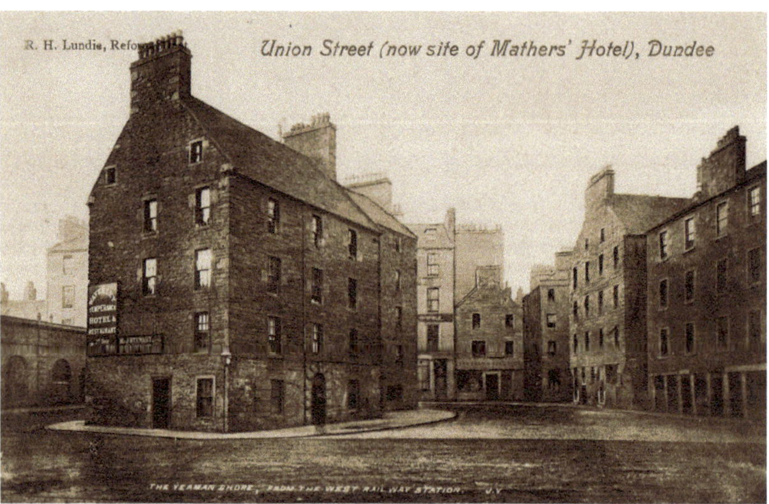

Cholera Hospital

In 1832 there was a devastating outbreak of cholera in Scotland. In Dundee more than 500 people died of the disease. This old building, which had once been used as the town's arsenal, was pressed into service as a cholera hospital. It was demolished to accommodate the new Whitehall Crescent. The caption on this postcard states that it was the site of Mathers Hotel (now Malmaison) but it mainly occupied what is now the area in front of the hotel.

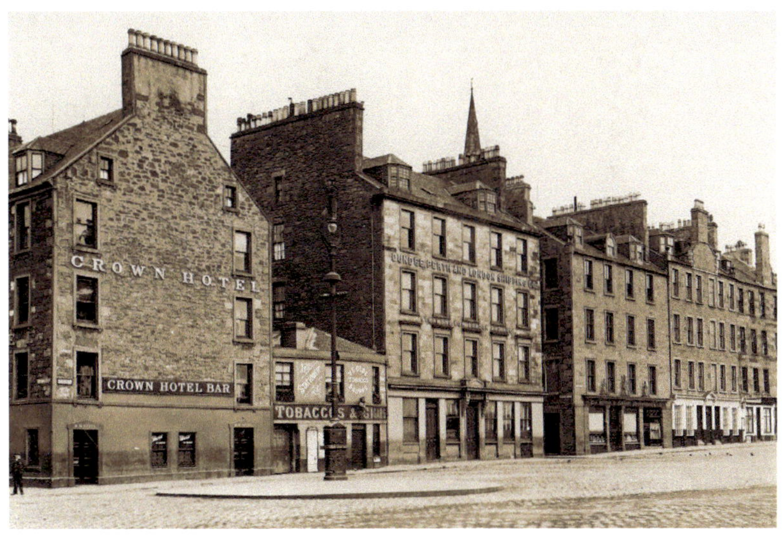

Shore Terrace Buildings

These buildings at Shore Terrace were demolished to make way for the Caird Hall. As can be seen, they included the headquarters of the Dundee, Perth and London Shipping Company, as well as the Crown Hotel. This was where, in 1909, a meeting was held to set up a new football club, Dundee Hibernian – later to become Dundee United. Also visible is the entrance to a lost street, Tindal's Wynd, an ancient route between the town centre and the river.

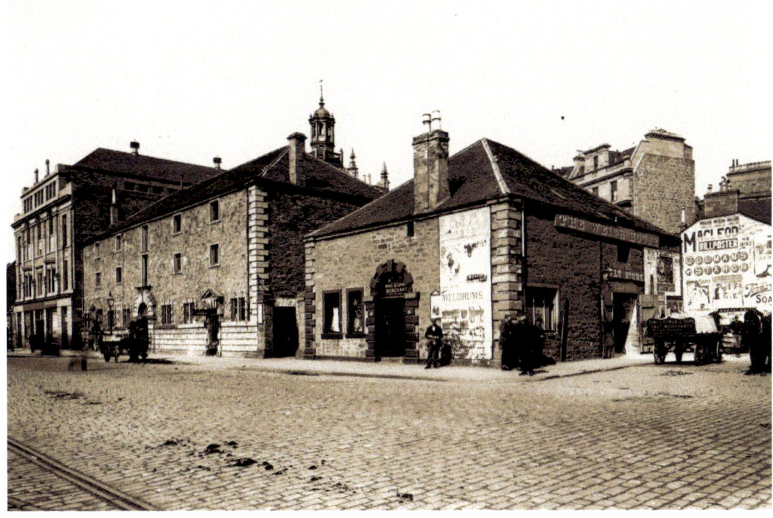

Dock Street Buildings

These buildings at Dock Steet were lost to the development of Whitehall Crescent. The proprietors of the wine and spirit merchant visible on the right of the picture were the Powrie family. In 1898, John Powrie took over the new pub that was built on the site – the Whitehall Bar (now the Bird and Bear). James Cowan and Sons, Salt Merchants, who shared the premises with the Powries, moved to new premises at No. 14 Dock Street (now Abandon Ship).

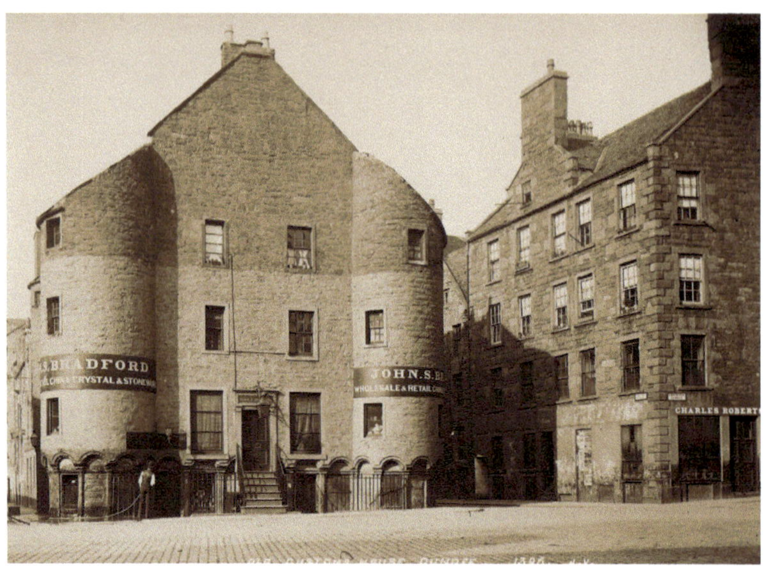

Provost Pierson's Mansion

This building was situated at the bottom of what is now Crichton Street. It is thought to have been built in the sixteenth century. It was constructed for John Pierson, who was Burgh Treasurer and later a bailie. His son James was provost from 1643 to 1646, earning it the name Provost Pierson's Mansion. In the eighteenth century, it was used as a Customs House and later as a store. It was acquired by the town council in 1878 and later demolished.

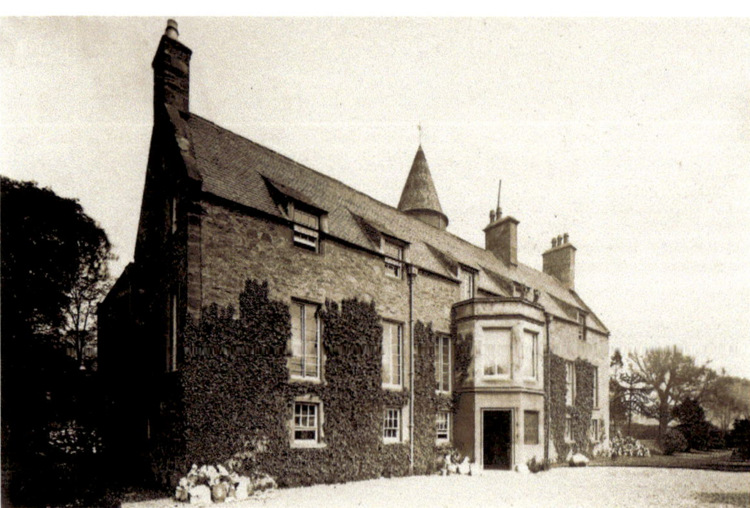

Blackness House

Blackness House occupied a space between present-day Peddie Street and Blackness Avenue. It was home to the merchant family the Wedderburns until the mid-eighteenth century when their Jacobite sympathies saw them lose the Blackness Estate and it come into the hands of the Hunter family. The name Blackness comes from the 'Black Ness', a rocky headland that once protruded into the River Tay near where the railway bridge now comes to land. Blackness House was demolished in 1930.

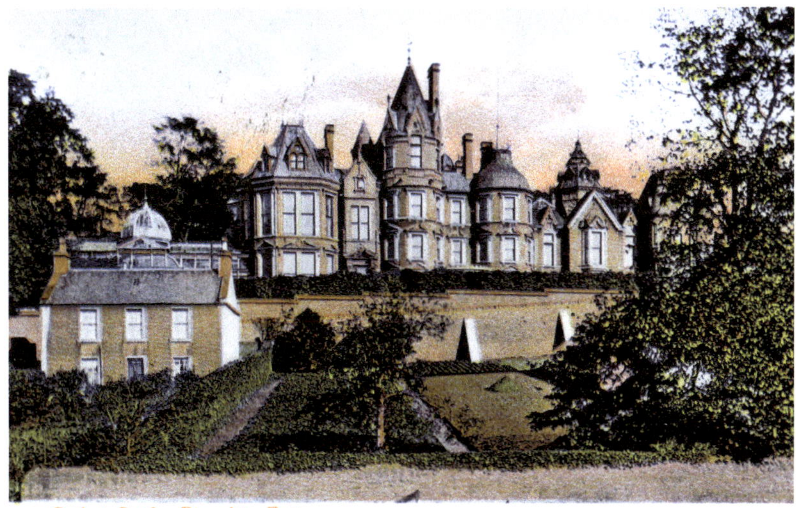

Carbet Castle

Kerbet House was purchased by Joseph Grimond of Bowbridge Works in 1861. He extended it in a French renaissance style to produce one of Broughty Ferry's famous 'jute palaces'– the mansions that Dundee's jute mill owners built for themselves away from the industrial city that they had created. Falling victim to dry rot, it was gradually demolished until only the west wing was left standing. This final section was demolished in 1984. Luxury flats have since been built on the site.

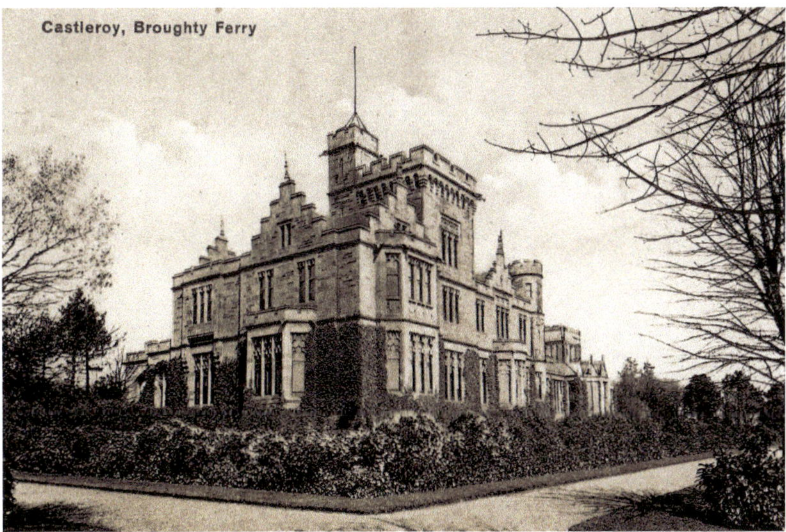

Castleroy

Castleroy was the largest and most flamboyant of the so-called jute palaces. It was built in 1867 for the Gilroy family, who owned Tay Works. It was said to have 100 rooms and 365 windows. During the Second World War it was used to accommodate Polish Forces. After the war, it was occupied by squatters. It came into the ownership of Dundee Corporation in 1946 but its dilapidated condition and dry rot led to its demolition in 1956.

2

Lost Streets

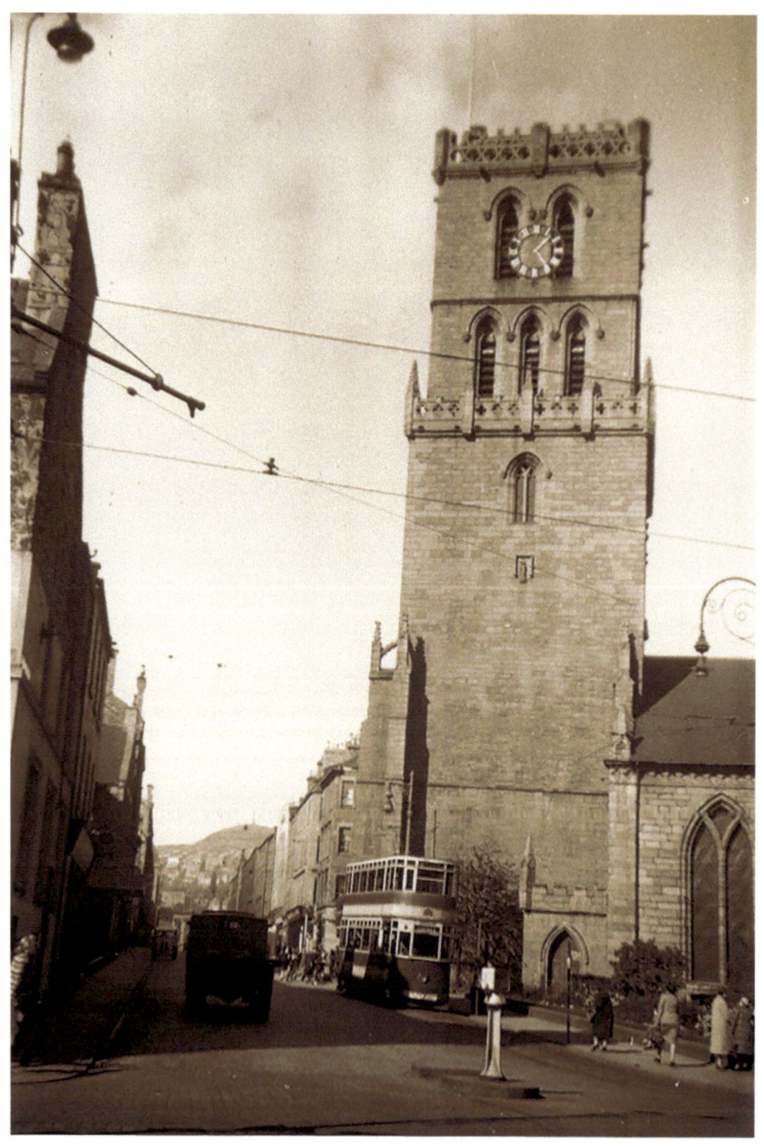

South Lindsay Street.

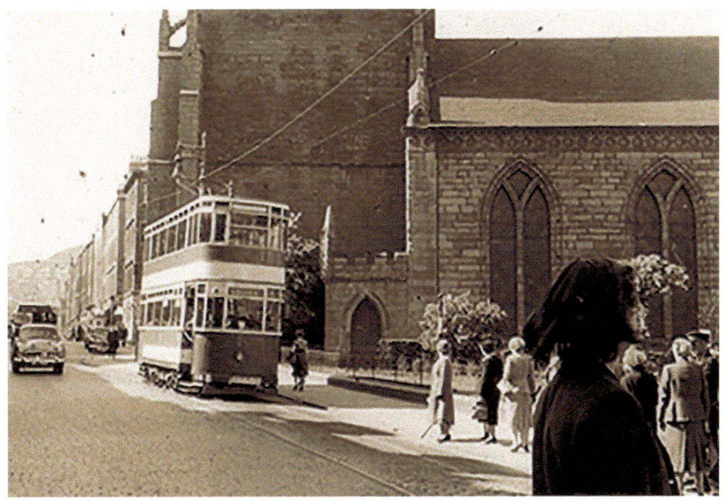

South Lindsay Street

While North Lindsay Street survives today, its southern counterpart vanished as part of the Overgate redevelopment of the 1960s. South Lindsay Street ran from the Nethergate, past the Old Steeple before crossing the Overgate to join with North Lindsay Street. It was the successor of School Wynd, which took its name from the location of the English School and the Grammar School. The new, wider street was named after William Lindsay, who was provost of Dundee from 1831 to 1833.

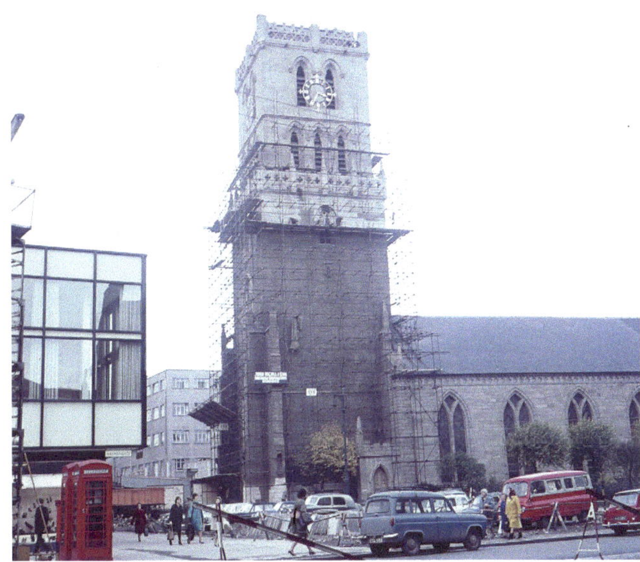

Old Steeple and Demolition of South Lindsay Street

While South Lindsay Street was being wiped from the map, Dundee's oldest building and greatest survivor, the Tower of St Mary, more commonly known as the Old Steeple, was undergoing a bit of a facelift. The tower dates from the fifteenth century, being completed around 1480. It has withstood the upheavals of the Reformation, several invasions of the town, a siege, the repeated destruction of the churches to which it is connected and even the 1960s developers.

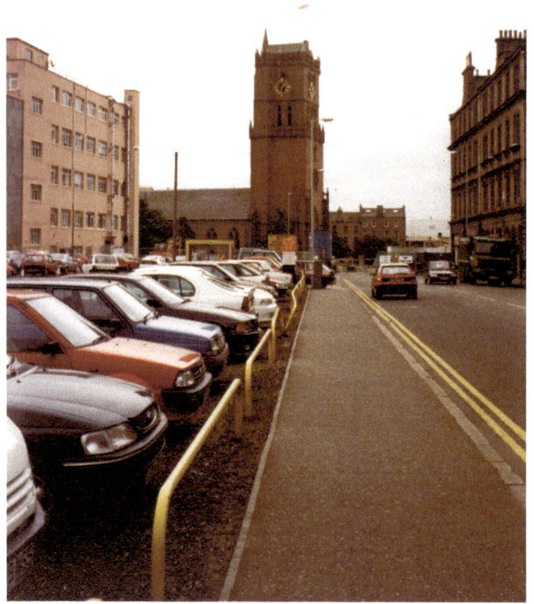

North Lindsay Street Looking to Nethergate

For a brief period at the start of the new millennium, following the demolition of the 1960s version of the Overgate, it was possible to have a clear view from North Lindsay Street to the Nethergate. North Lindsay Street was once the site of Corbie Hill (otherwise Windmill Brae, so called because it had been the site of a windmill). The hill was quarried away to the extent that by 1831 North Lindsay Street could be built there.

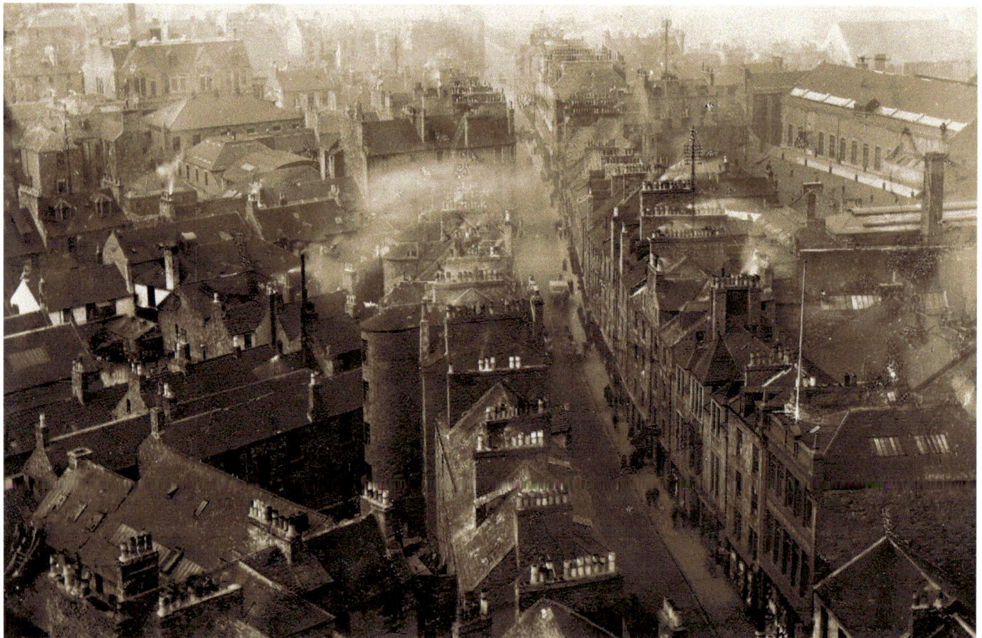

Overgate

The Overgate is undoubtedly Dundee's most famous lost street. The ancient thoroughfare began as the Argyllgait in the earliest days of the burgh. In the sixteenth century it became known as the 'over' or high road or 'gait' as opposed to the lower or nether gait. This view from the top of the Old Steeple looks towards the West Port and beyond to the Hawkhill in a seamless progression which would be destroyed by the redevelopments of the 1960s.

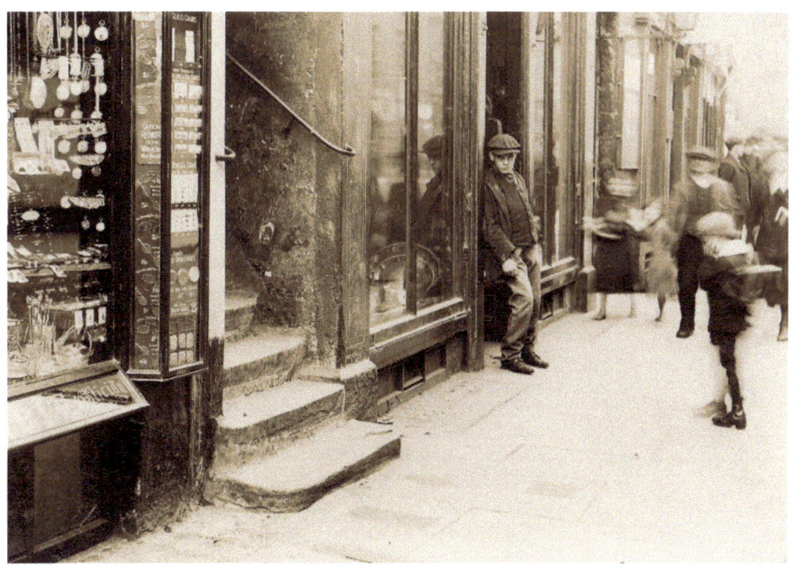

Overgate

The High Street end of the Overgate around the beginning of the twentieth century. A young man tries to outstare the camera, causing himself to remain in focus as opposed to the blurred appearance of the passers-by. At the left side of the picture is the window where William Petrie established a business as a jeweller, watchmaker and optician at No. 9 Overgate in 1895.

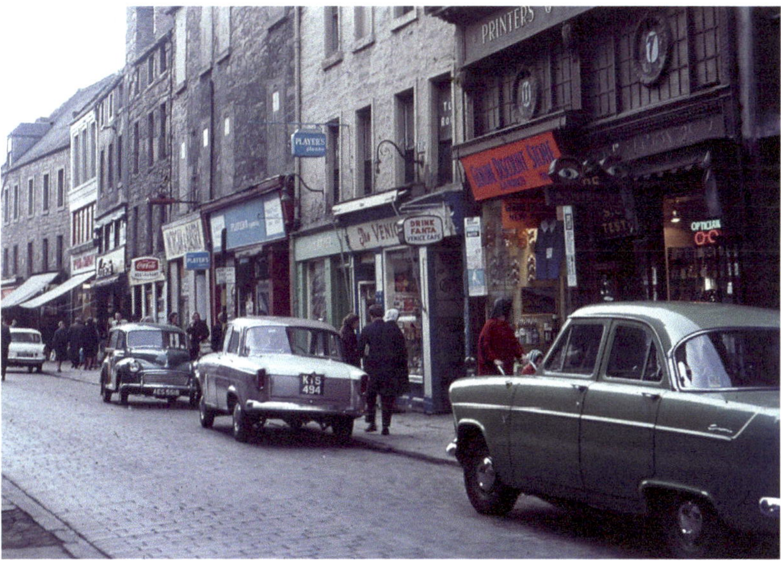

Overgate

The close entrance and shop window that are on the left of the photo above are on the right of this one, which was taken in the early 1960s. William Petrie's shop is still there, though Petrie himself had retired in 1950 after fifty-five years and sold the business to Ernest W. Brown. At the time this photograph was taken most of the Overgate had been demolished, leaving only this section.

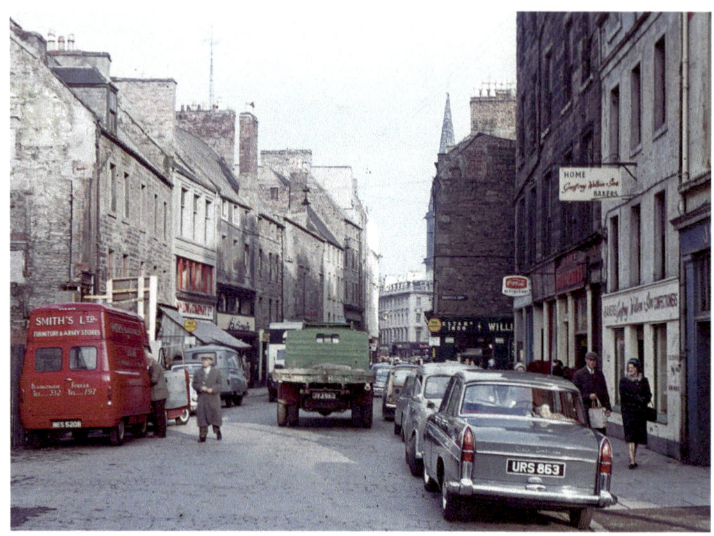

Thorter Row

Looking from the Overgate back towards the High Street. Visible going off to the right of the picture is Thorter Row. It was known by this name from the fifteenth century until its demolition in the 1960s – supposedly because it ran between or 'athwart' the High Street and the Overgate. Tradition also has it that it was here that General Monck's massacre of the town's inhabitants in 1651 was stopped, by the sight of a child suckling its murdered mother.

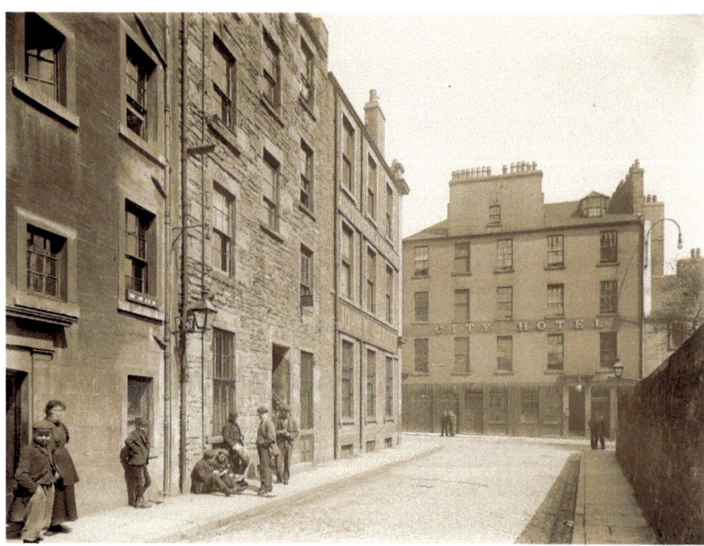

Mid Kirk Style

Mid Kirk Style was a narrow street running from Tally Street to Lindsay Street between the Overgate and the City Churches. This view looks towards Tally Street (see next page). In its latter years, Mid Kirk Style was famous for its markets and particularly for the sale of 'busters', a combination of chips and mushy peas said to have been introduced to Dundee by the De Gernier family, who were originally from Belgium.

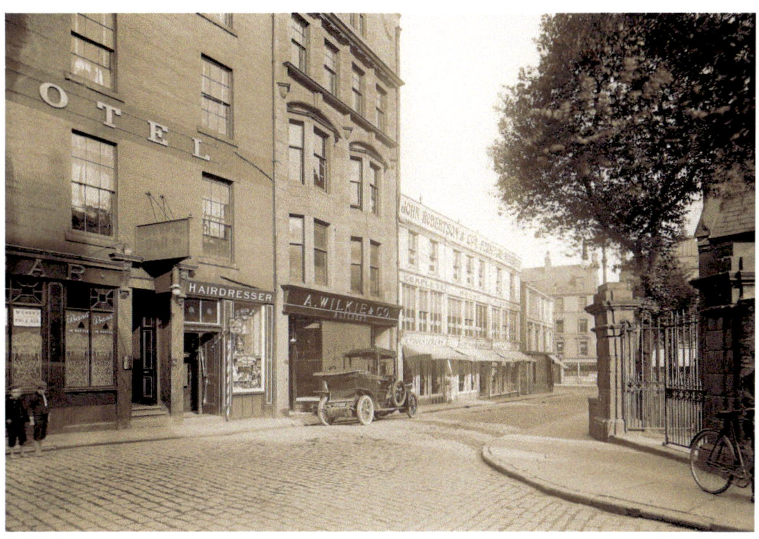

Tally Street

On the right-hand side of this view of Tally Street looking down from the Overgate towards the Nethergate is a glimpse of the entrance to the City Churches, which may help the modern viewer to determine its location. This image dates from the early years of the twentieth century. Cars were few and far between on Dundee's roads at this time and were the preserve of the rich. This one belonged to local businessman and jute merchant Charles B. Ovenstone.

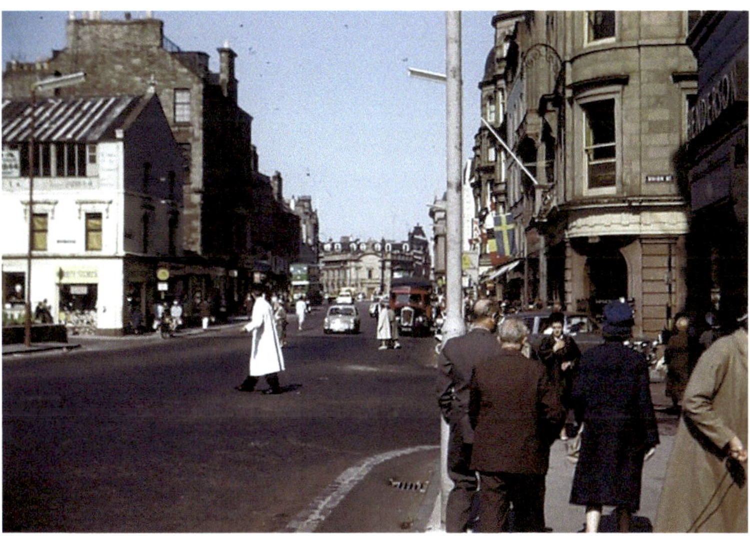

Tally Street from Nethergate

This 1960s view of the Nethergate shows the location of Tally Street from the other side, marked by the white building on the left. This building along with most on that side have been demolished while the right-hand side is largely unchanged. Like several streets in the area, Tally Street vanished with the construction of the first Overgate Centre around this time but a pedestrianised approach to the current Overgate Centre from the Nethergate marks its approximate location.

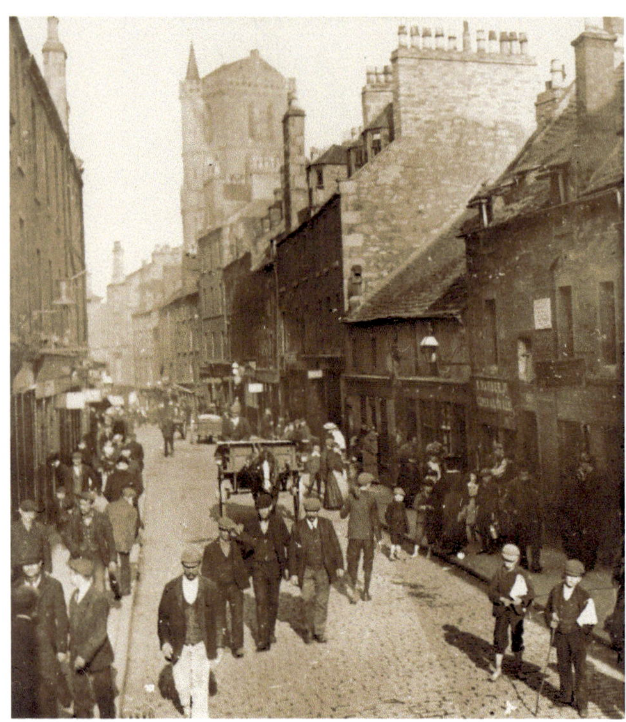

Overgate Looking to Lindsay Street

Whereas the current version of the Overgate Centre comes to an abrupt end where it meets the main road on its western side, the original street continued beyond Lindsay Street until it met the north and south sections of Tay Street and the West Port. So completely has this section of the Overgate been wiped from the map that it is only the survival of the Old Steeple that enables a modern viewer to get their bearings.

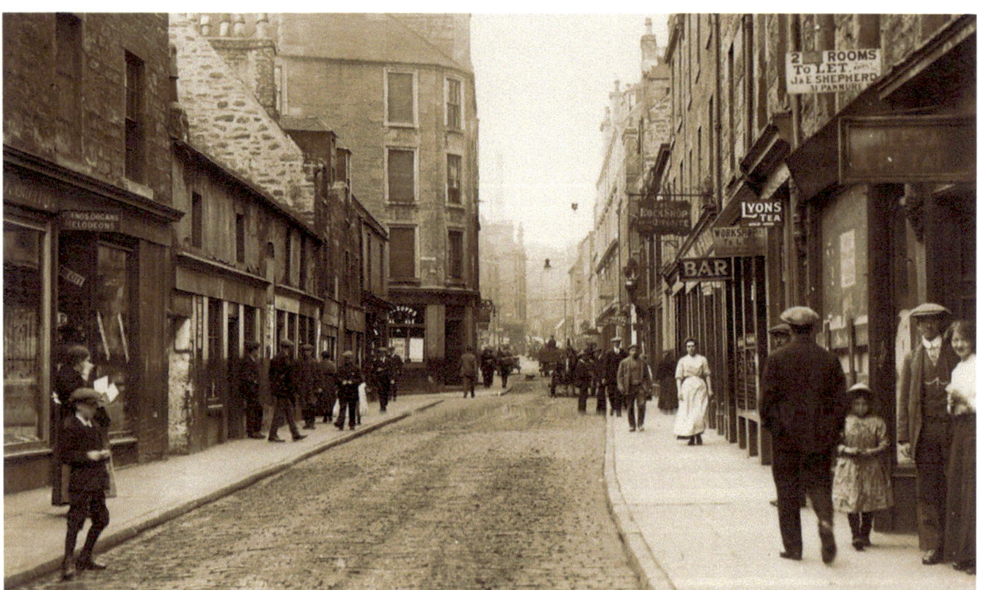

Overgate Looking to West Port

A little further along the Overgate, this time looking in the opposite direction towards the West Port, with the Hawkhill in the distance. Going off to the left is Long Wynd, which ran from the Overgate down to the Nethergate where it emerged next to St Enoch's Church. The buildings in the distance at Temple Lane and the beginning of Hawkhill remain in place.

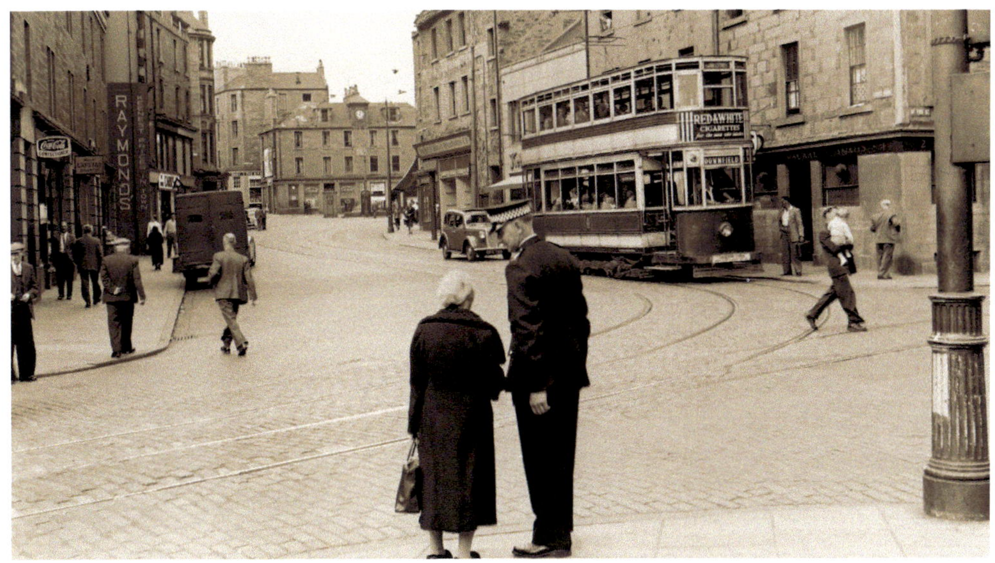

West Port

The West Port takes its name from one of the gateways in the city walls which once stood in the vicinity, though it is believed to have actually been located a little further back, near the top of Long Wynd in the Overgate. The West Port survives today but has changed a lot since this photograph was taken in 1955. All of the buildings on the right were demolished to allow for road realignment.

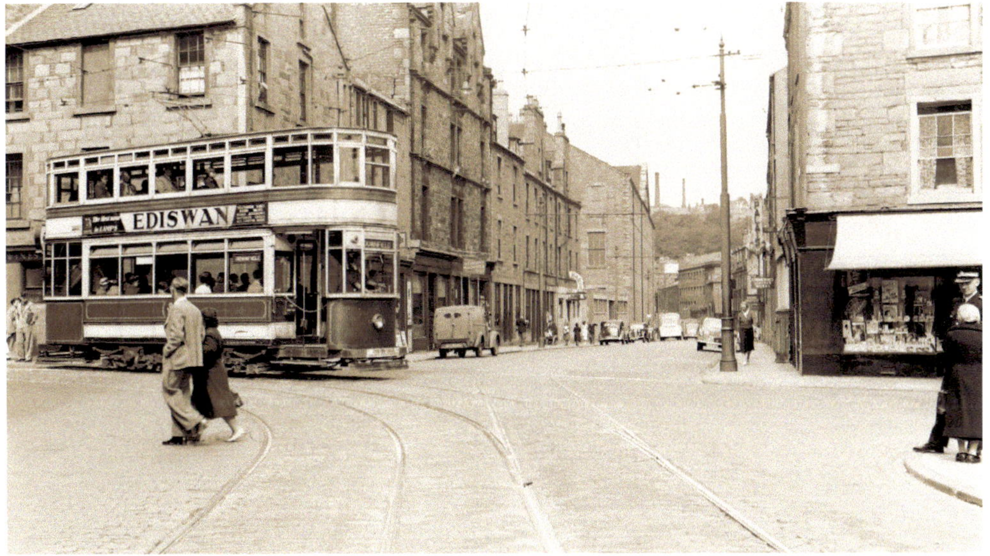

North Tay Street

The police officer and the woman who were in conversation in the centre of the previous photograph remain in the same place in this one, but now appear on the right-hand edge of the frame as the photographer has moved. He is now looking straight down another lost street, North Tay Street. The former Tay Works at Marketgait can be seen in the distance.

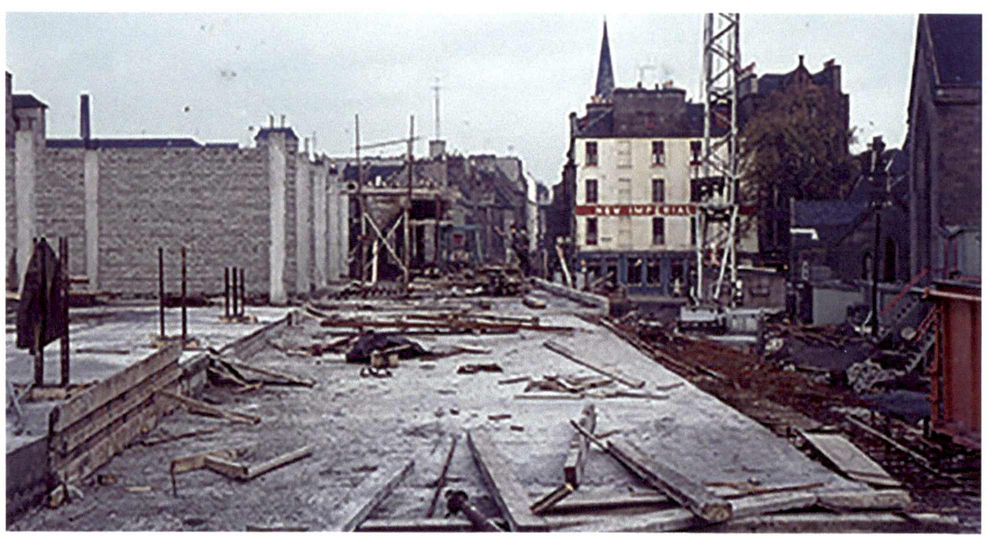

Building the 1960s Overgate Centre

The 1960s Overgate Centre was designed by Ian Burke, Hugh Martin & Partners. It was built in three phases. Phase one was concerned with the western end of the shopping centre and the Angus Hotel and phase three focused on the High Street end. This picture shows the construction of phase two – the central pedestrian precinct with an upper tier of shops and a car park on the roof. The surviving section of the old Overgate is visible in the distance.

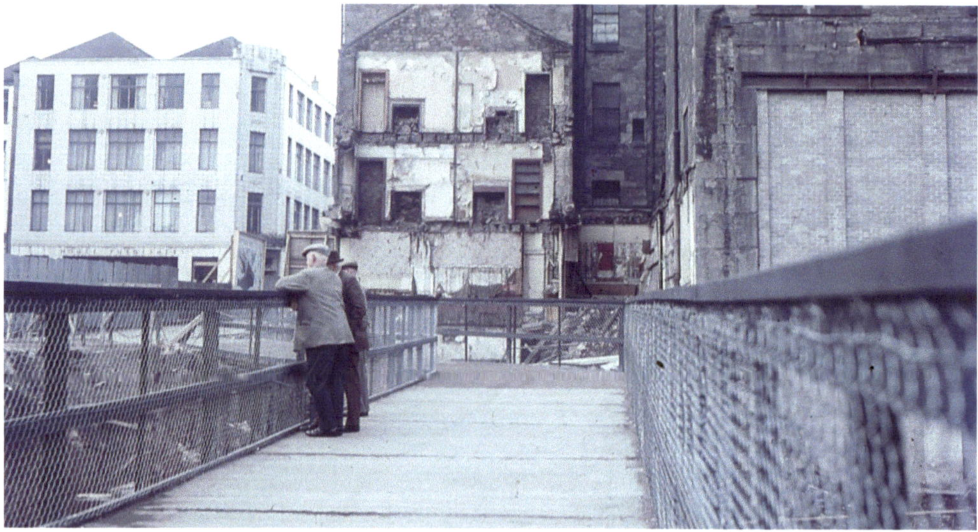

Demolition of the Overgate

These men are most likely witnesses to the destruction of the Overgate area as they have known it for their whole lives and as it has been known for generations before that. Thay are standing in what is left of the area that was bounded by the Overgate, North Lindsay Street, Willison Street and Barrack Street. The remaining buildings on the right of this view were also later demolished and Robertson's furniture store on the left was, as we have seen, destroyed by fire in 2022.

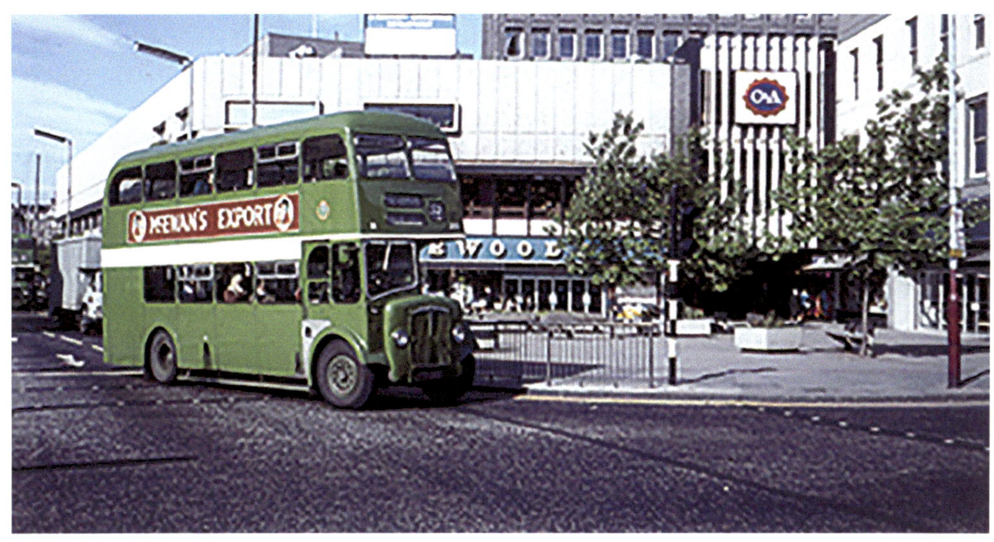

Overgate

A view of the 1960s Overgate redevelopment from the High Street showing popular shops of the period. C & A took its name from its Dutch founders Clemens and August Brenninkmeijer. Littlewoods was founded in Liverpool by John Moores in 1923 as a football pools organisation that later moved into mail order. The popular Littlewoods restaurant is visible on the first floor and advertised to customers in the lower window. A green Dundee Corporation bus completes the scene.

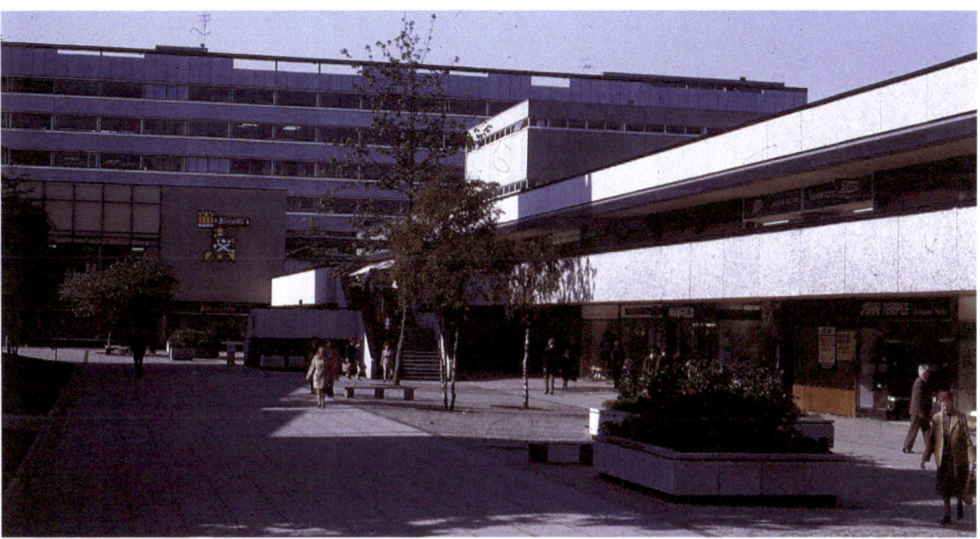

Overgate

Another view of the new Overgate in the 1960s, this time looking towards the Angus Hotel, showing the centre's two shopping levels. Prominent here is Birrell's shoe shop. The firm of A. Brirrell and Sons was founded in 1867 and had been at No. 107 Overgate (at the corner of the Overgate and North Lindsay Street) since that time. Just short of a century later, they moved into this brand-new shop near the site of the old.

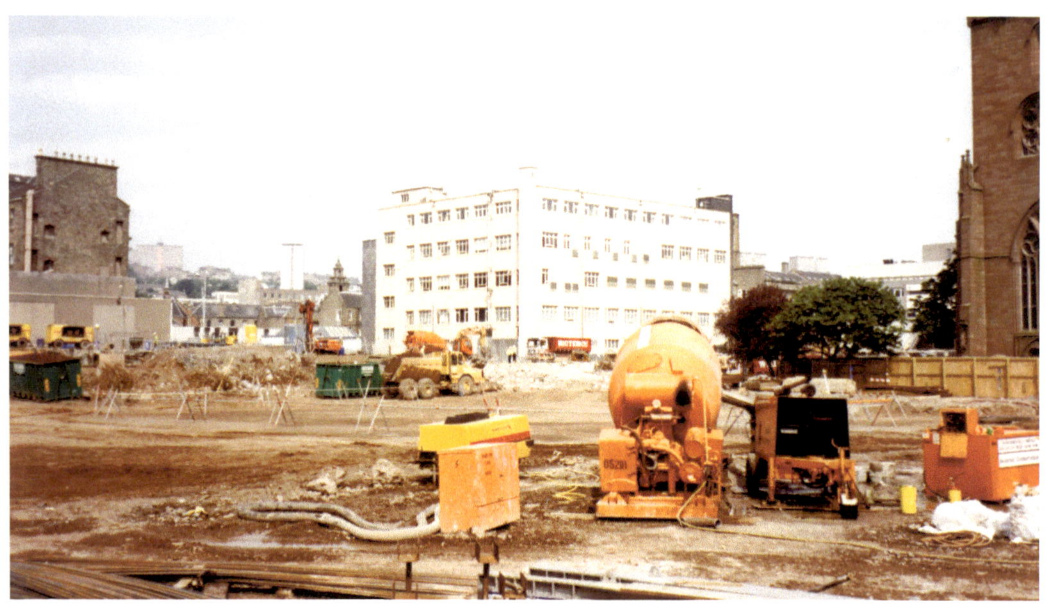

Demolition of the Overgate

Less than forty years after the demolition of the old Overgate, the shopping centre which replaced it was also demolished to be replaced with the present version. This photograph shows the cleared site looking towards Willison Street. A glimpse of the great survivor among Dundee buildings, the Old Steeple, on the right-hand side of the image provides a further guide to the location.

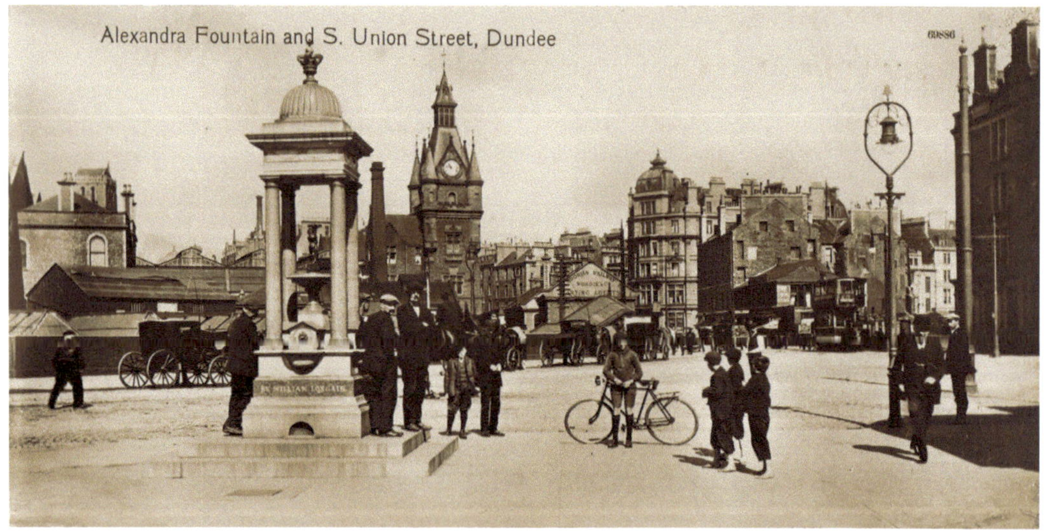

South Union Street

The works surrounding the construction of the Tay Road Bridge had the effect of severing the natural connection between the city and the River Tay. The continuity between Union Street and its southern counterpart became lost and the area became a patchwork of roads and pedestrian walkways. The twenty-first century redevelopment of the waterfront area has effectively restored South Union Street.

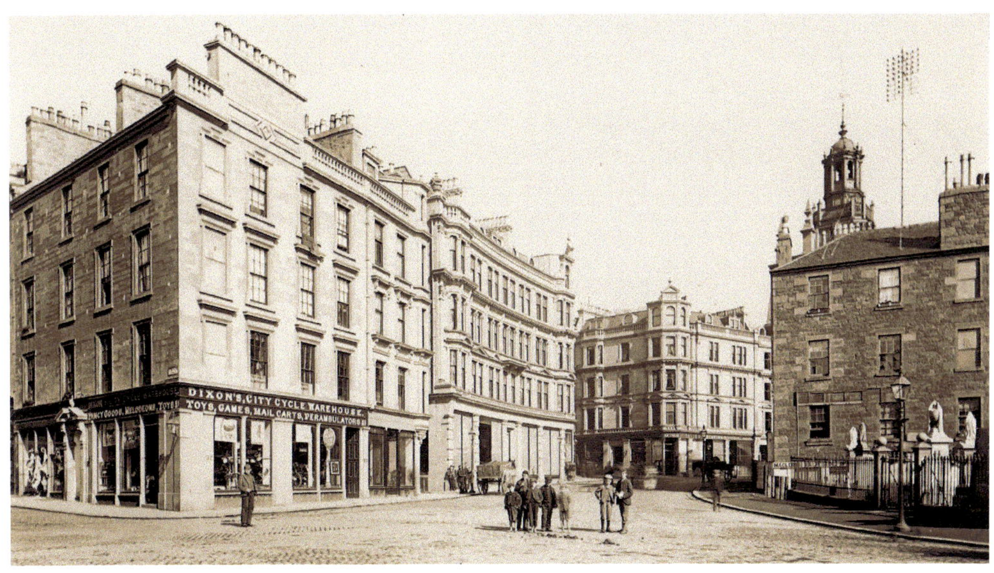

South Union Street

Another view of South Union Street near its junction with the northern part of the street. This scene remains recognisable today with the most glaring difference being the absence of Mather's Temperence Hotel (now the Malmaison), which opened at the turn of the twentieth century. The gravestones visible to the right of the scene do not signify the site of a forgotten cemetery but rather the yard of Joseph Fairweather, a monumental sculptor.

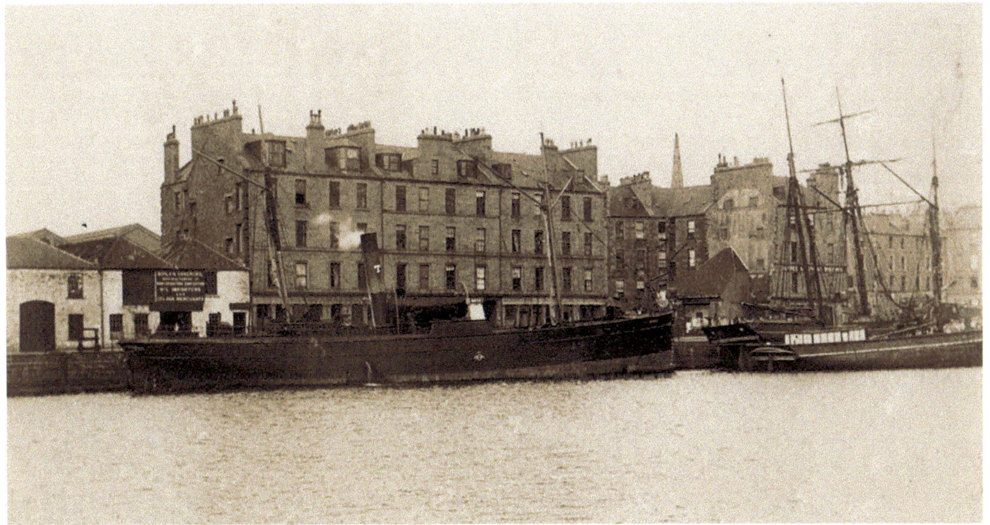

West Dock Street

This late nineteenth-century view looks across the Earl Grey Dock to West Dock Street, which ran down the west side of the dock from Dock Street itself towards the West Protection Wall, arriving at what would today be the middle of the V & A. Another lost street – Craig Street – ran between West Dock Street and South Union Street.

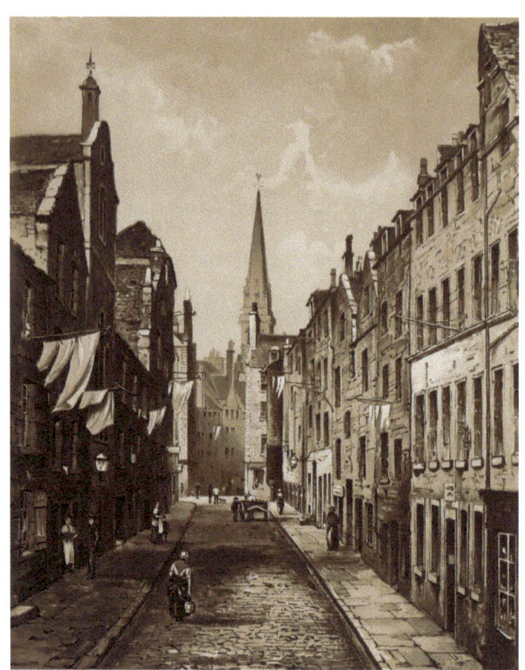

Fish Street

Fish Street ran from the foot of Union Street to the Greenmarket at the bottom of Crichton Street where it emerged to the north of Provost Pierson's mansion. Its tall buildings were once owned by leading families and its occupants respectable, but by the mid-nineteenth century it had become an area of ill repute. It was demolished along with Butcher Row to make way for Whitehall Cresent.

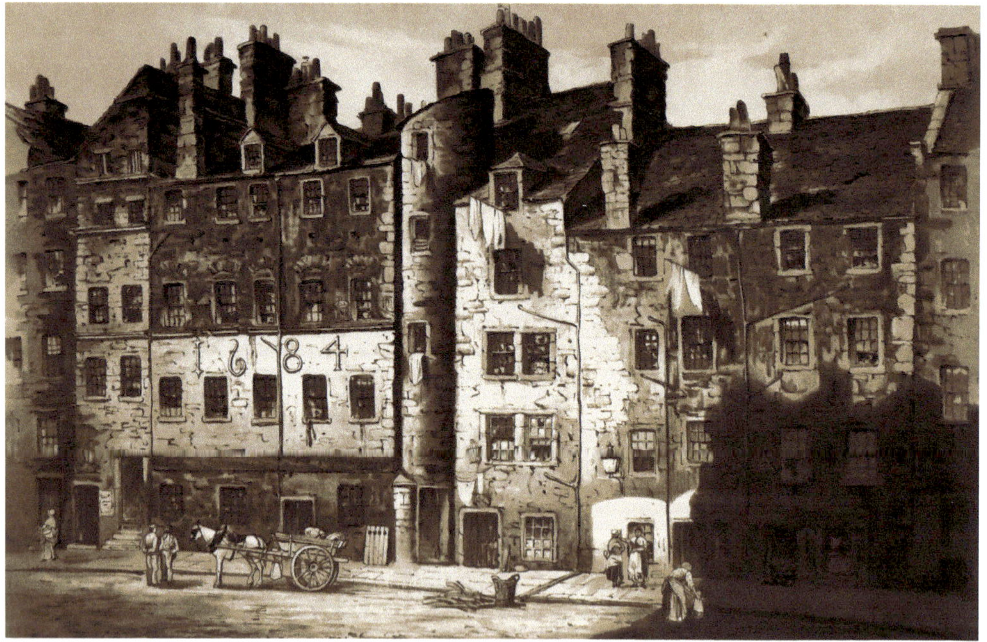

Butcher Row

Butcher Row was built around the sixteenth century on reclaimed land in front of Fish Street and was originally known as the New Shore. It was of superior appearance to the more haphazard Fish Street. It gained its later name when the town's flesh market relocated to the area from the High Street in 1776 when the Trades House was built on its former site.

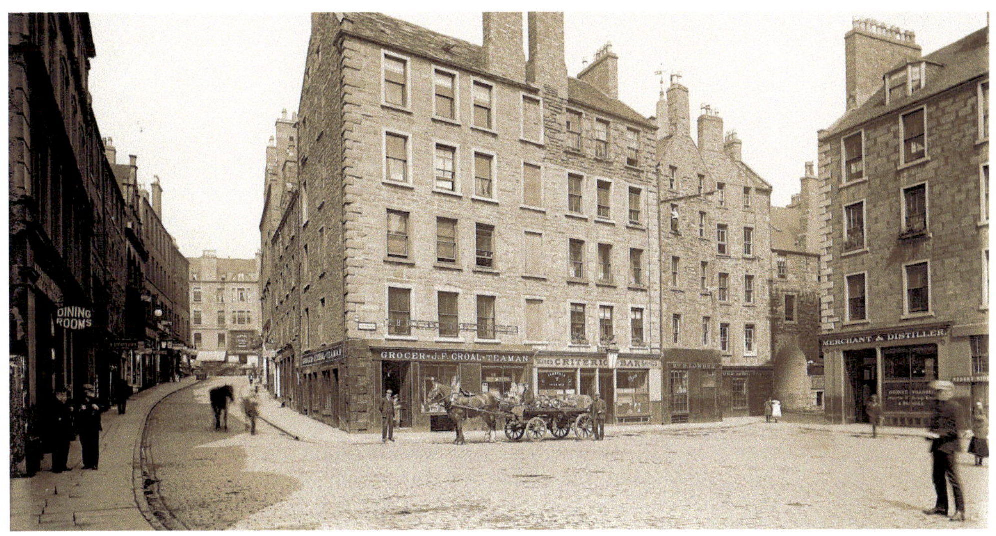

Greenmarket

A search for the Greenmarket in Dundee today will point you to an area between the Nethergate and Riverside. However, in the nineteenth and early twentieth centuries, it referred to this area at the foot of Crichton Street between the Vault and the docks, which was a regular venue for markets and fairs. After the construction of the Caird Hall on much of the site, markets and travelling shows continued to visit the reduced space now known as Shore Terrace.

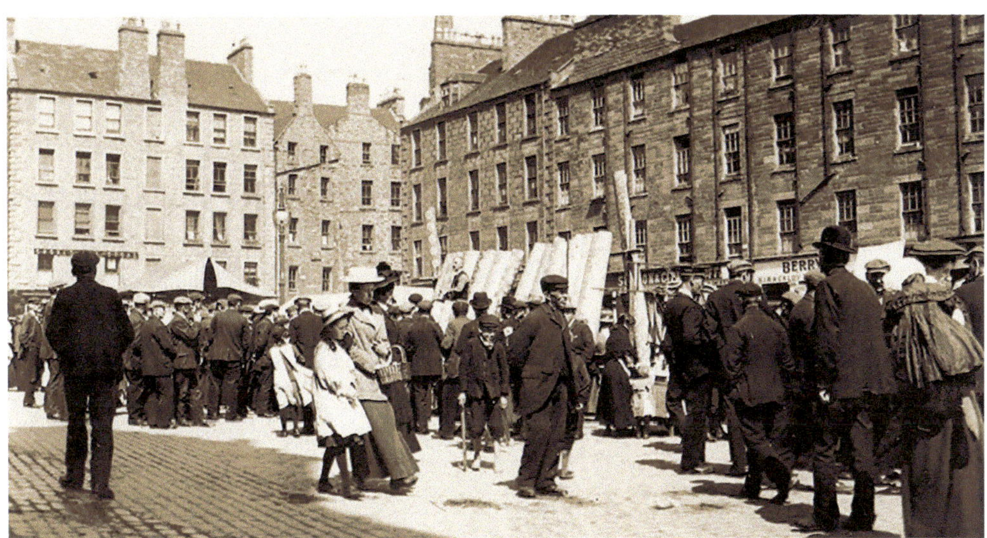

Greenmarket

The Greenmarket was the kind of place you could buy anything – particularly noticeable in this picture is the linoleum seller. Fishwives from as far away as Arbroath would bring seafood to Dundee to sell. There was also a Lemon and Kali man who sold kali – a type of crystal sherbet. A corruption of this word left generations of Dundonian children calling sherbet 'Kelly'. It was here too that that chips were first sold by the Belgian Edward De Gernier.

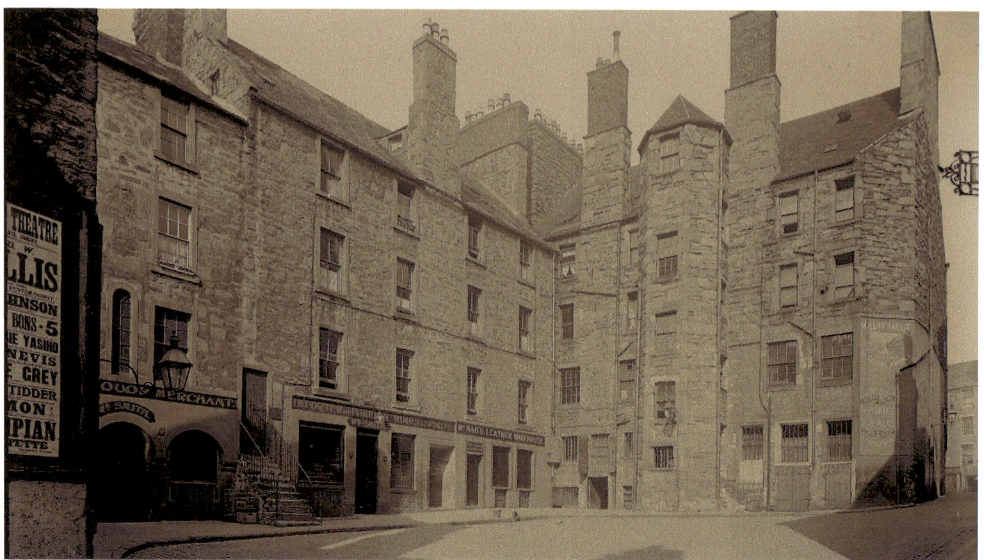

The Vault

The Vault ran down from the High Street behind the Town House to meet St Clement's Lane, which started at the other side of the building. The poster for the People's Palace in the Nethergate dates the photograph to May 1904 when Fred W. Millis, an Australian ventriloquist, topped the bill, which also featured a comedian with the unlikely name of Ben Nevis. The entire area was demolished to make way for the City Square and Caird Hall.

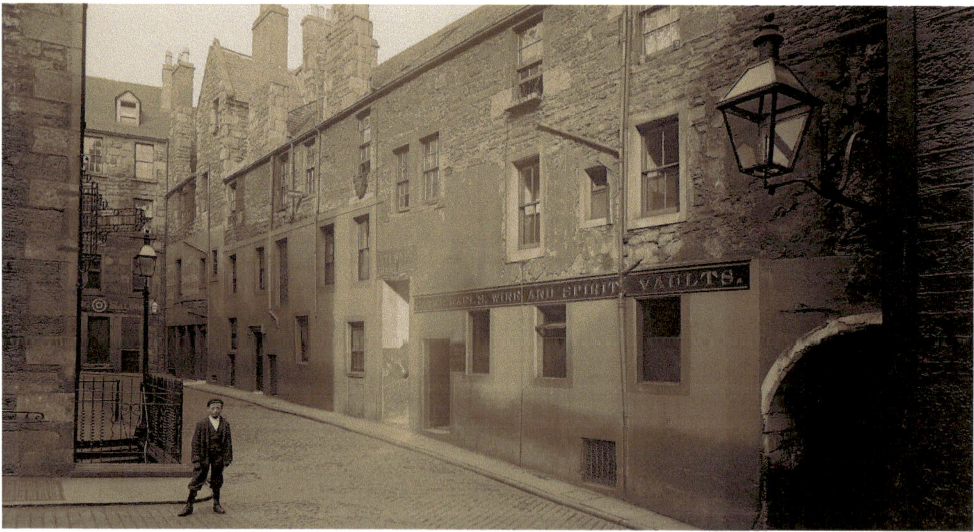

St Clement's Lane

St Clement's Lane is shown here where it meets the Vault. The name commemorates St Clement's Church, which once stood where the City Square is today and which was Dundee's main burying place until 1567 when Mary Queen of Scots gifted the ground that became the Howff. The archway shown here, which gave the Vault its name, led to another lost street, Castle Lane, where it met the Greenmarket.

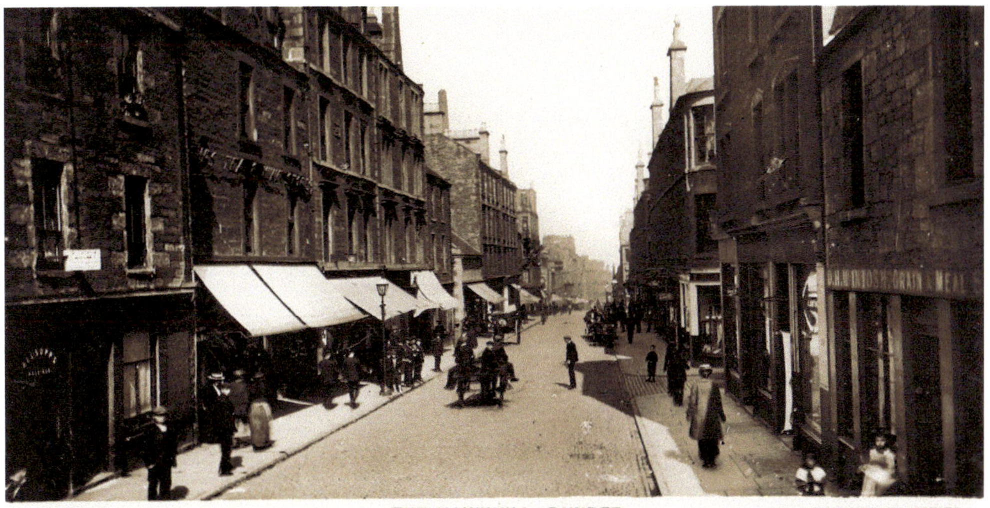

Hawkhill

The Hawkhill might not, strictly speaking, be a lost street as part of it survives under the name Old Hawkhill and another part joins on to the main road which now bears the name. The once thriving and densely populated community shown in this old postcard view, though, is definitely a thing of the past. All of the buildings in this view have gone and the area is dominated by buildings connected with the University of Dundee.

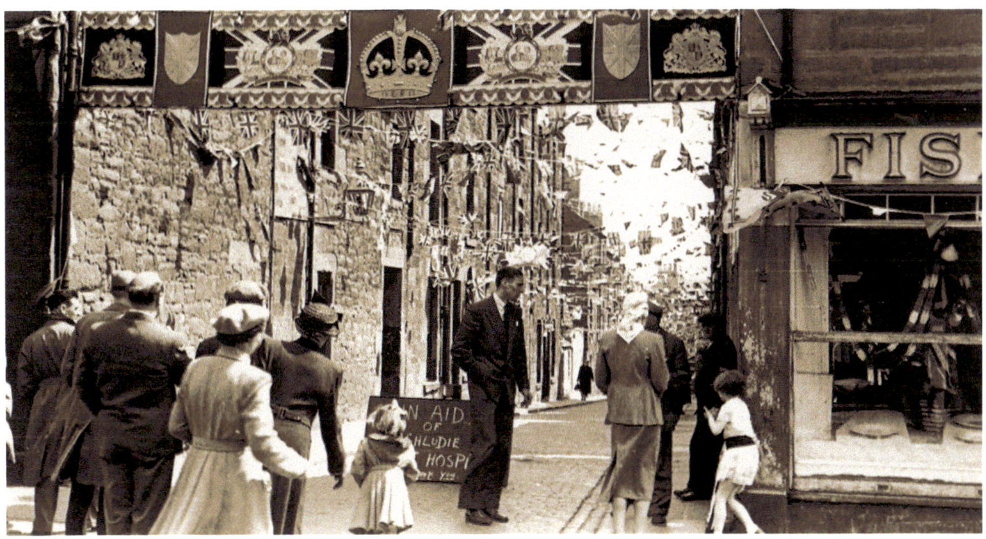

Bernard Street

Bernard Street was a narrow side street off the Hawkhill. It became well known in Dundee for being festooned with flags and other decorations at the time of national events. The tradition began during the Silver Jubilee of King George V in 1935. The street also celebrated the Coronation of King George VI in 1937, VE Day and VJ Day in 1945, the King and Queen's Silver wedding in 1948 and, seen here, the Coronation of Queen Elizabeth in 1953.

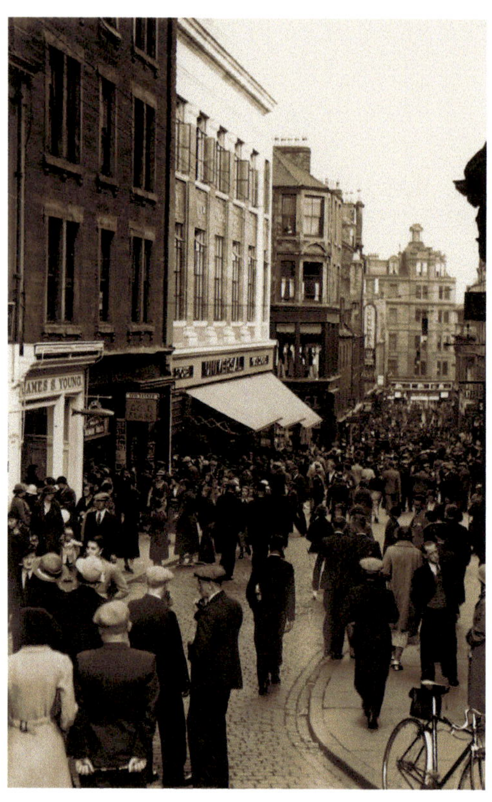

Wellgate, 1930s

The Wellgate rose from the Cowgate via the steps at the top, to the foot of the Hilltown. It was the 'gait' or way to the Lady Well, which was located there and was for centuries Dundee's principal source of drinking water. Its use was granted by Sir James Scrymgeoure of Dudhope in 1409. The street is shown here in the 1930s.

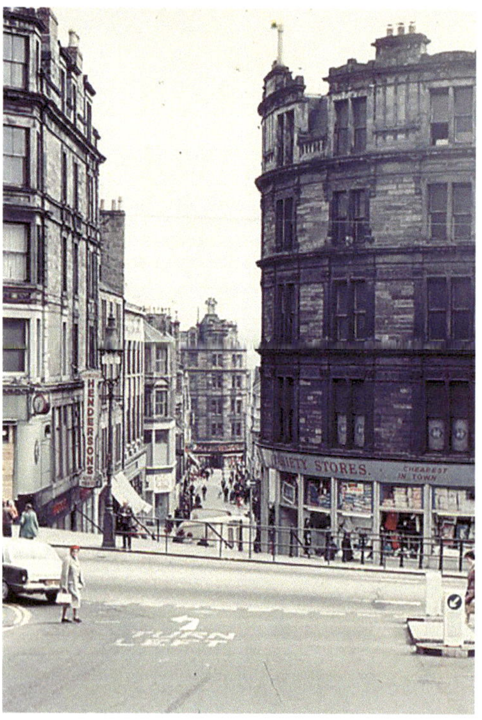

Wellgate, 1960s

By the time this photograph was taken in the late 1960s, the Wellgate was still a popular shopping street, if not quite as crowded as in the previous view. It was demolished in the early 1970s to make way for a new shopping centre, which was given the name the Wellgate Centre. The original Wellgate Steps are beyond the railings in this image. They were replaced with a new version following the completion of the shopping centre.

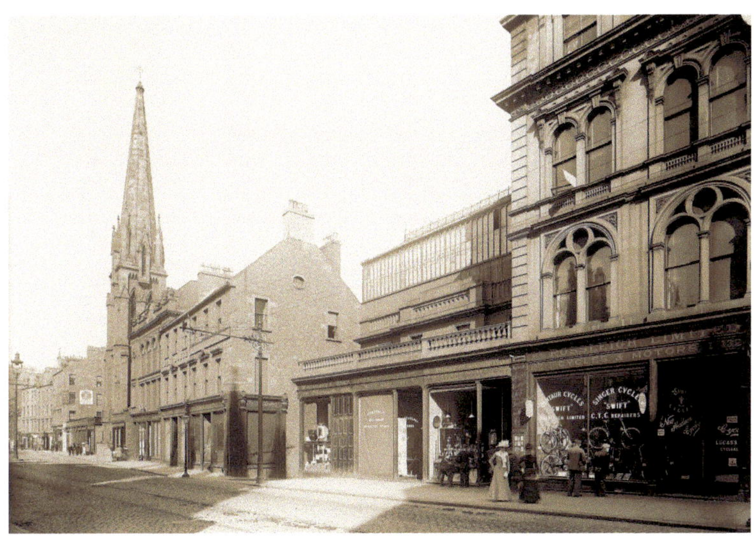

Sea Wynd

Everything between St Paul's Church and the cycle shop in this image has now been replaced by the inner ring road, which now cuts through the once seamless progression from the High Street to the Perth Road, splitting the Nethergate in two. This includes Sea Wynd, an ancient route which ran from the Nethergate to Yeaman Shore. The cycle shop itself is now home to Groucho's pub having previously been the Dundee institution Groucho's Record Exchange.

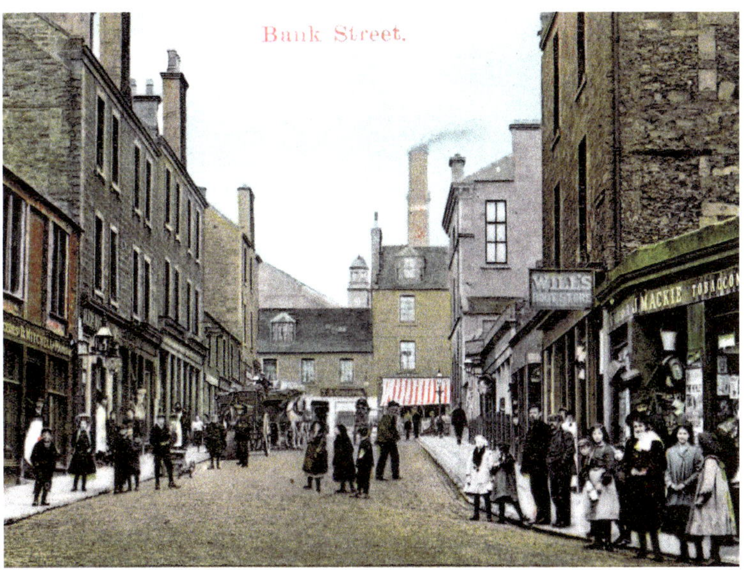

Bank Street, Lochee

Bank Street once linked the Lochee High Street to South Road. Redevelopment of this side of the High Street in the 1970s saw Bank Street disappear from the map. It has reappeared in more recent years, but not quite in its original location and catering for modern traffic means that the once organic connection with South Road is now interrupted by a dual carriageway and a roundabout.

3

The World of Work

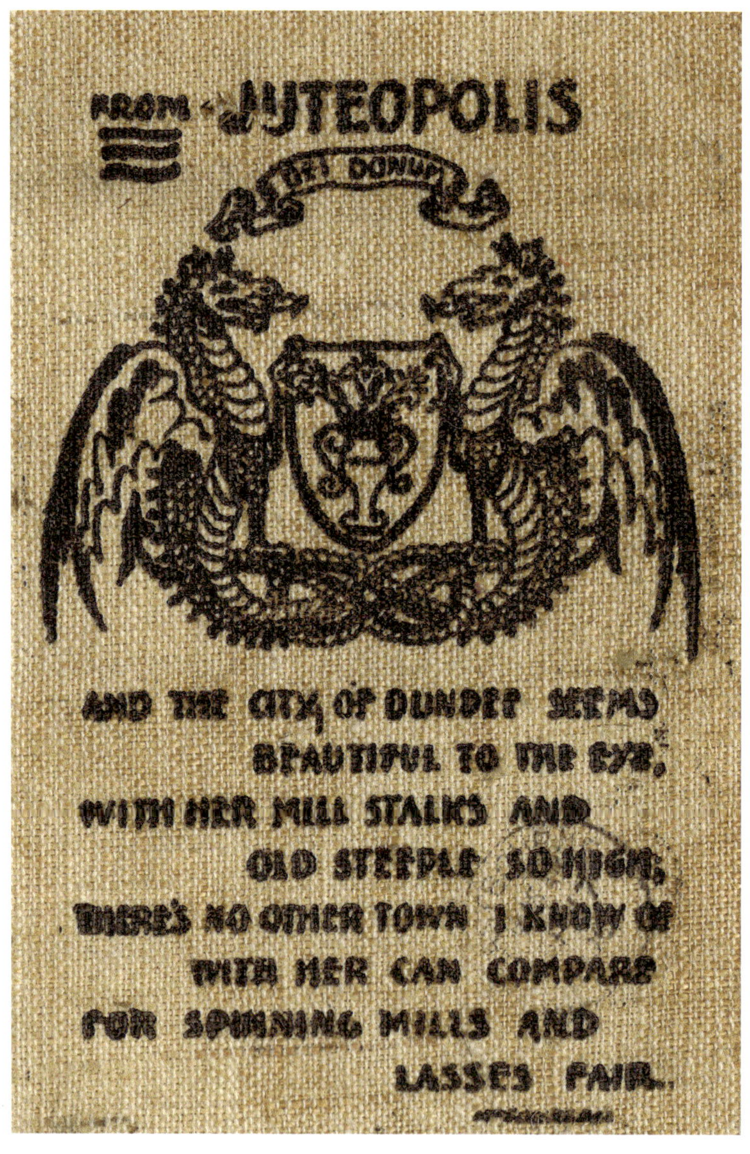

Jute-fronted postcard celebrating Dundee's most famous industry.

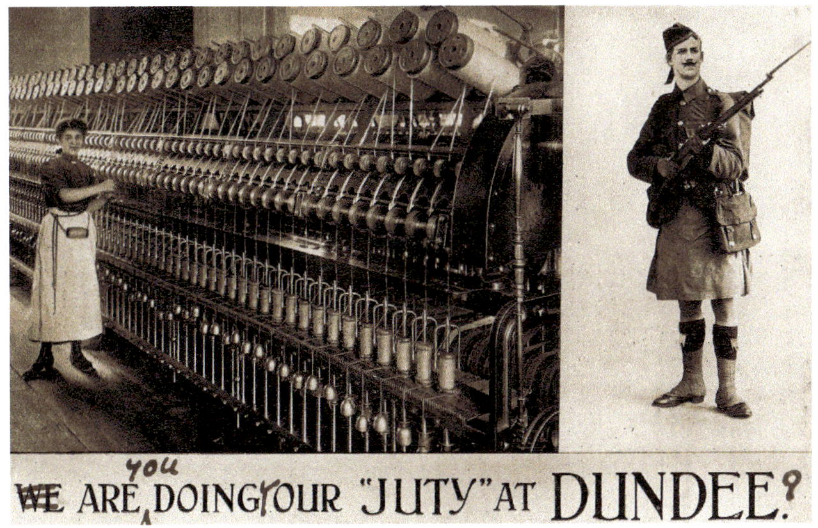

Jute Industry

Dundee was known for its three Js – jute, jam and journalism. Jute was the most important of these and the industry was largely responsible for the expansion of Dundee in the nineteenth century. The jute plant itself was grown in India and processed in Dundee. This postcard dates from the time of the First World War and shows how much Dundee was associated with the industry at the time. The sender has changed the caption to pose a question.

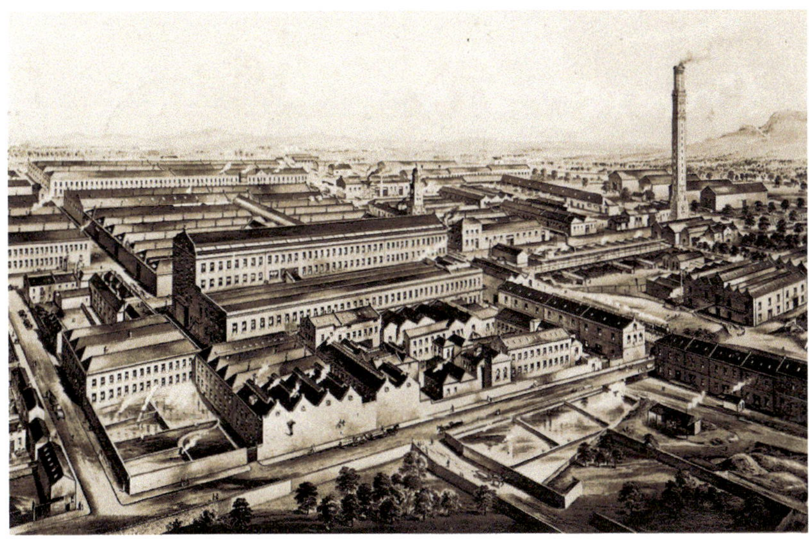

Camperdown Works

Camperdown Works was the home of jute manufacturers Cox Brothers Limited in Lochee and was constructed in stages from 1850. The High or Silver Mill was built between 1857 and 1868 and included a 100-foot clock tower at its eastern end. Eventually, the works had its own railway branch, foundry, stables and half-time school. The most notable feature was, and remains, the 282-foot-high brick chimney, known as Cox's Stack, which was built between 1865 and 1866.

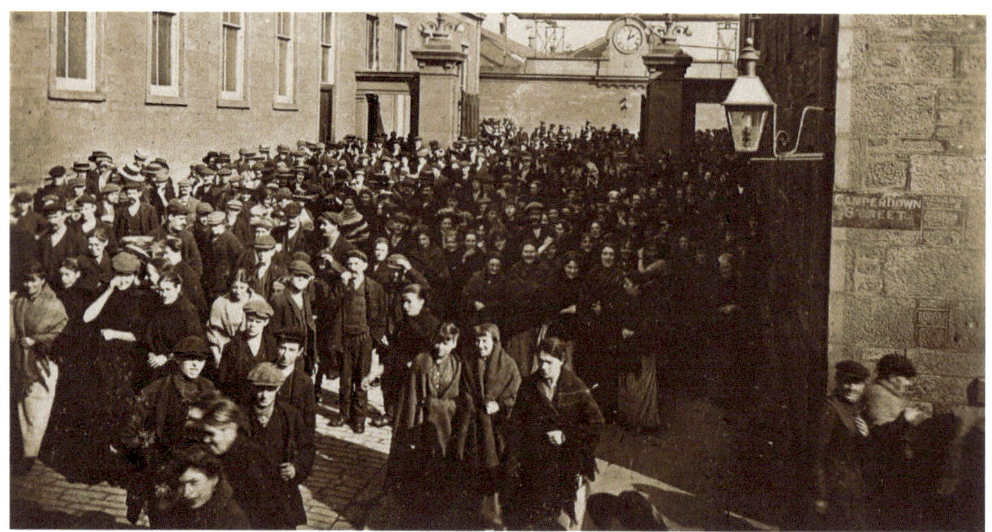

Workers Leaving Camperdown Works

Around the time this photograph was taken around 5,000 people worked at Camperdown Works. Several times a day there would be an exodus of workers through the gates into Methven Street and into Lochee High Street as their shifts ended. It is little wonder that Lochee became a thriving area when the mill was at its height. By the time the works closed in 1981, however, there were only 340 workers left.

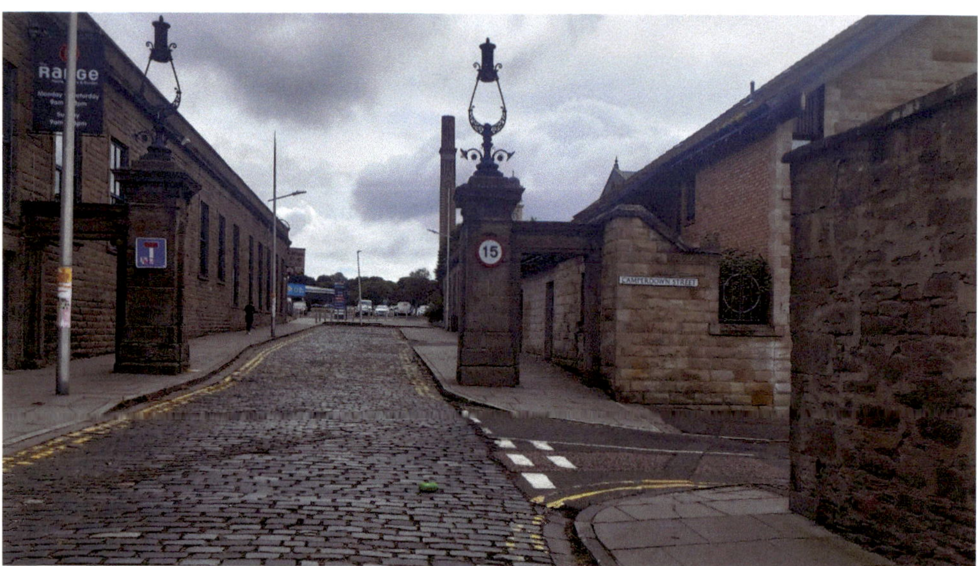

Methven Street Today

Today most of the site of Camperdown Works is the Stack's Leisure Park. The High Mill has been converted to housing. Cox's Stack, robbed of its original function, stands as a memorial to Dundee's lost industrial heritage. If it seems incredible that the space between the gates and the opening of Camperdown Street could accommodate the number of people shown in the previous image, then that is because the gateposts have been moved forward.

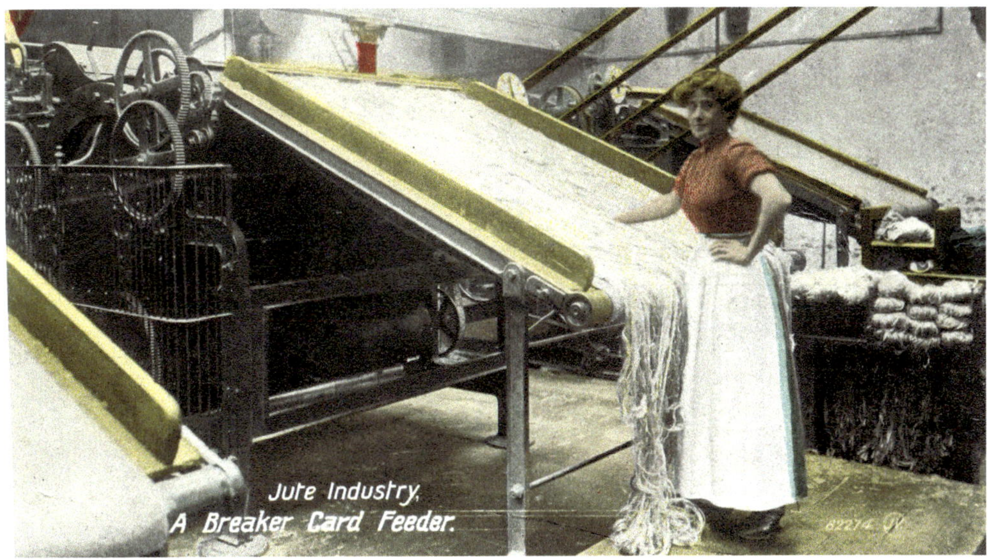

Breaker Card Feeder

This is part of a series of postcards showing different stages of the jute manufacturing process. Carding is the process of separating the jute fibres in preparation for spinning. The jute would be fed through hackle-covered cylinders, which would deliver the fibres in the form of a ribbon or sliver, which was formed into a roll at the breaker card and packed into a can at the finisher card.

Keiller's Marmalade

Janet Keiller ran a small confectionery business in the Dundee's Seagate in the eighteenth century. The traditional story is that her husband John bought a cargo of Seville oranges at Dundee harbour which were too bitter to eat and she created her own spin on an existing recipe for a type of jam by adding strips of orange rind. Keiller's is certainly believed to have been the world's first commercially produced marmalade. Janet is also credited with popularising Dundee Cake.

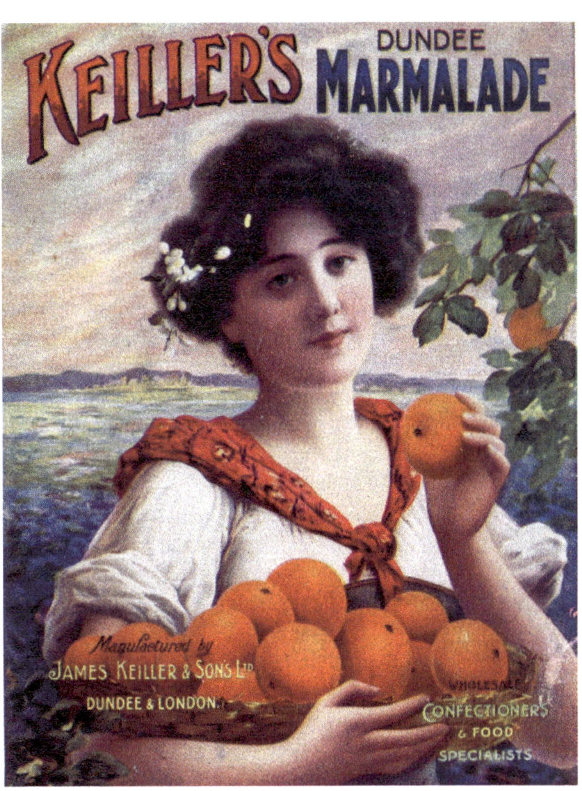

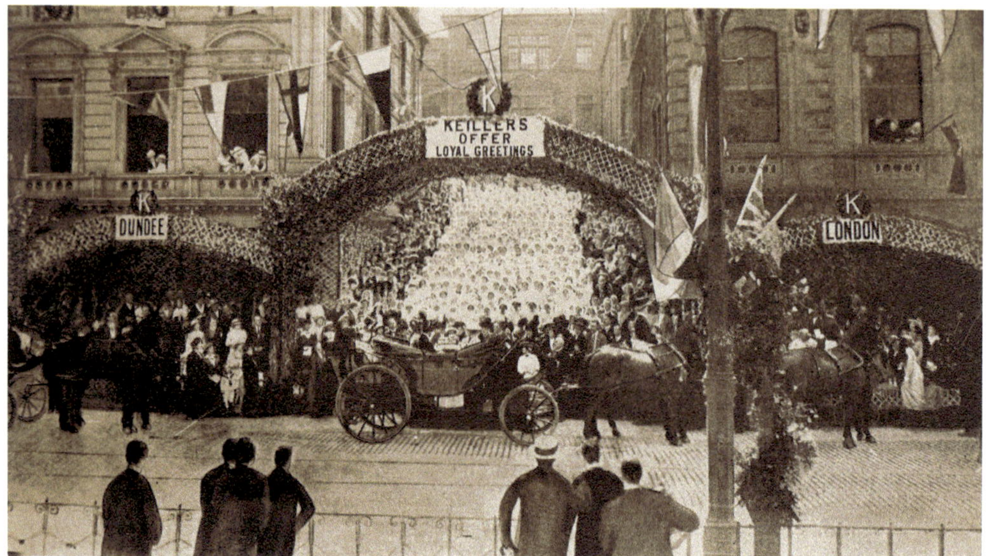

Keiller's Factory

By the middle of the nineteenth century the Keiller family business had expanded to operate a large factory located between the High Street and Albert Square. The entrance at Chapel Street is seen here dressed as an orange grove to represent the company's most famous product for the visit of King George V and Queen Mary in 1914. The factory closed in the 1970s and was replaced by a shopping centre, which was given the name the Keiller Centre.

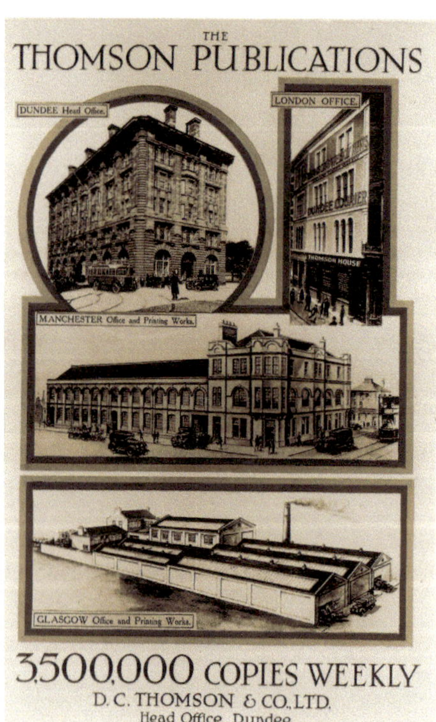

D. C. Thomson

The third 'J' in Dundee's three Js was journalism and the prime exponent of this remains D. C. Thomson, famous for publications including the *Beano* and the *Sunday Post*. The company was founded by David Couper Thomson in 1905, though his father William had taken control of the *Courier and Argus* in 1886 and several of the company's publications long predate this. The phenomenal success of Thomson's publications in the early twentieth century can be seen in this advertising postcard.

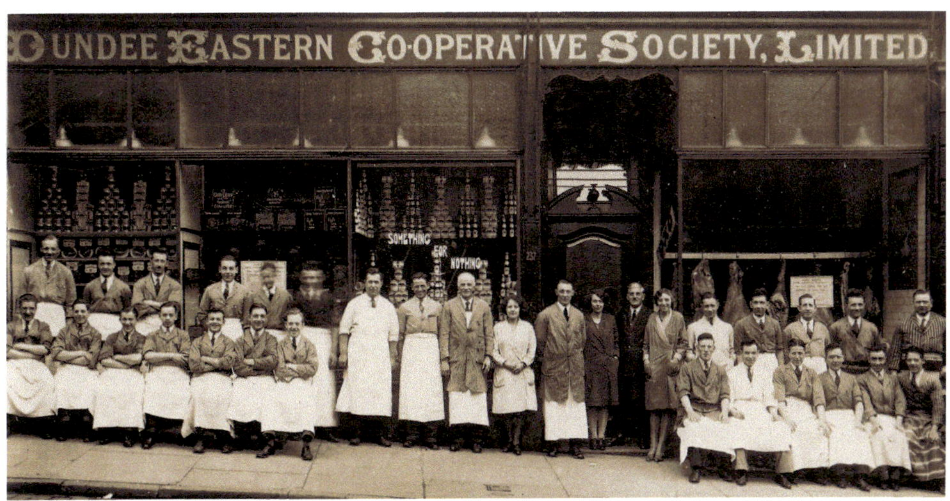

Dundee Eastern Co-operative Society

Known locally as 'the Sosh' – believed to be a corruption of the word 'society' – branches of the Dundee Eastern Co-operative Society were once common throughout Dundee and employed a large number of people as this photograph shows. As can probably be deduced from the slope of the ground, this branch was located on the Hilltown and was, in fact, just uphill of North George Street. It is interesting to note that 'something for nothing' is being advertised in the window.

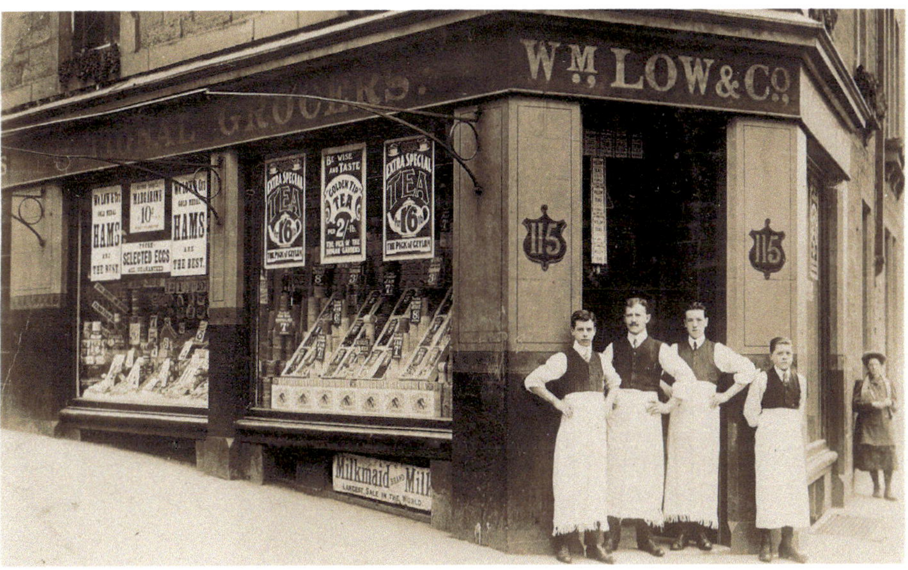

William Low and Co.

William Low began work in the grocery store that his elder brother had opened in Hunter Street in 1868. He bought the business in 1879. By the turn of the century, there were sixty-four William Low stores in Scotland. There were branches across Dundee including this one at Albert Street. The firm successfully managed the transition to supermarkets. In 1994, however, the business was taken over by Tesco and the name of 'Willie Low's' disappeared from Dundee's streets.

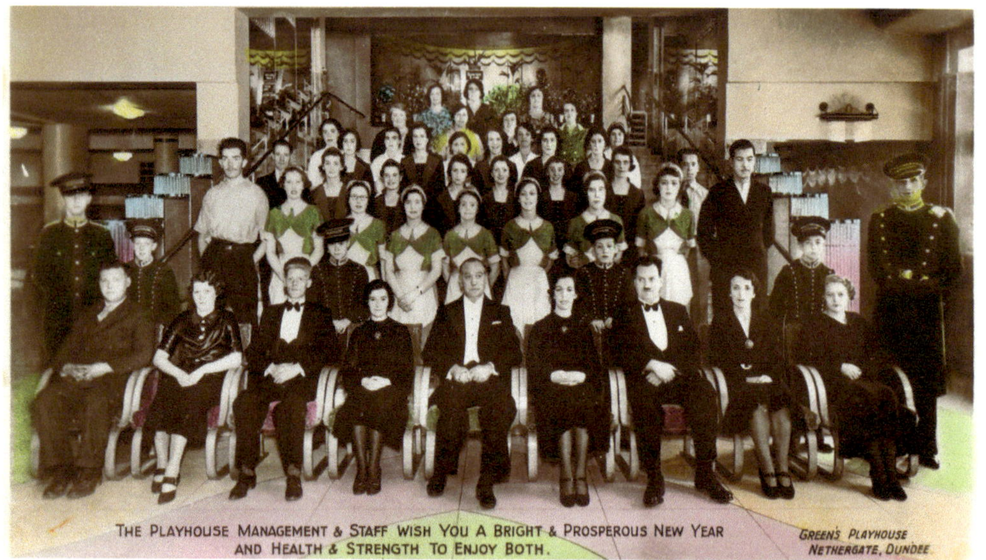

Green's Playhouse Staff

The large number of cinemas in Dundee meant that this sector provided employment for many. This picture shows the staff of Green's Playhouse assembled for a Christmas photograph in the late 1930s. Green's employees did not have to travel far for staff dances as a combination of the spacious foyer and the dance floor in the café meant that they did not have to leave the premises.

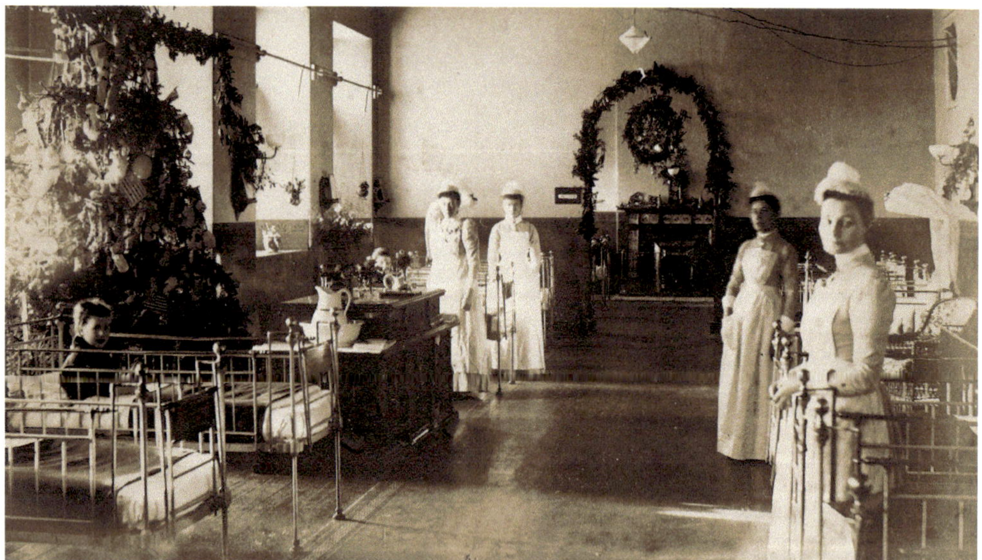

Nurses at Dundee Royal Infirmary

One profession that was traditionally open to women was nursing. These nurses and their patients are shown in the children's ward of Dundee Royal Infirmary at Christmas 1891. The infirmary opened in 1855 with accommodation for 220 patients and was one of the first to separate medical, surgical and fever wards. It replaced an earlier hospital building in King Street, which had opened in 1798.

Female Tram Conductor

The period of the First World War and the consequent shortage of male workers saw women begin to be employed in many areas where they had not worked before. This was true even in Dundee, which was long used to women working in the jute industry and often being the main breadwinner. It was not until 1917 that it was agreed to start employing women as conductors on the Dundee trams, however, and this photo dates from around that time.

Postman

This postman was obviously proud enough of his uniform to be photographed in it. The photograph was taken in a studio at Crescent Lane. His headgear dates the image to the early part of the twentieth century as this military-style cap was discontinued in favour of flat peaked caps in the late 1920s. The workwear of Dundee's modern-day posties may not be so photogenic but is considerably more practical.

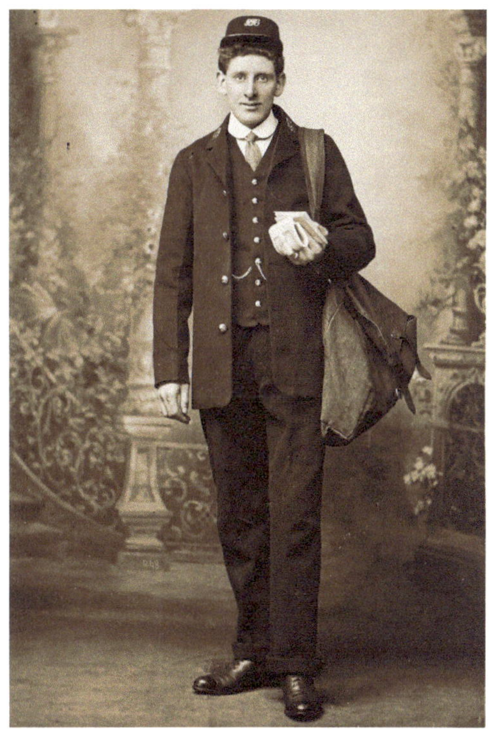

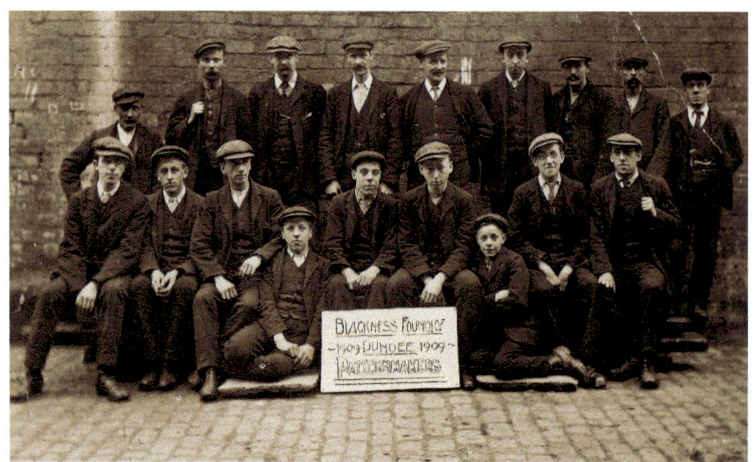

Blackness Foundry Workers

Blackness Foundry was constructed in the late 1860s for Urquhart Lindsay and Company, who were mill engineers and textile machinery manufacturers. It was founded in 1865 by Joseph Lindsay and William Walton Urquhart. The company later merged with Robertson and Orchar, becoming Urquhart, Lindsay and Robertson Orchar. They, in turn, were acquired by Messrs. Fairbairn Lawson Combe Barbour Limited of Leeds and Belfast. The foundry closed in 1958. The building was used as a warehouse before being demolished.

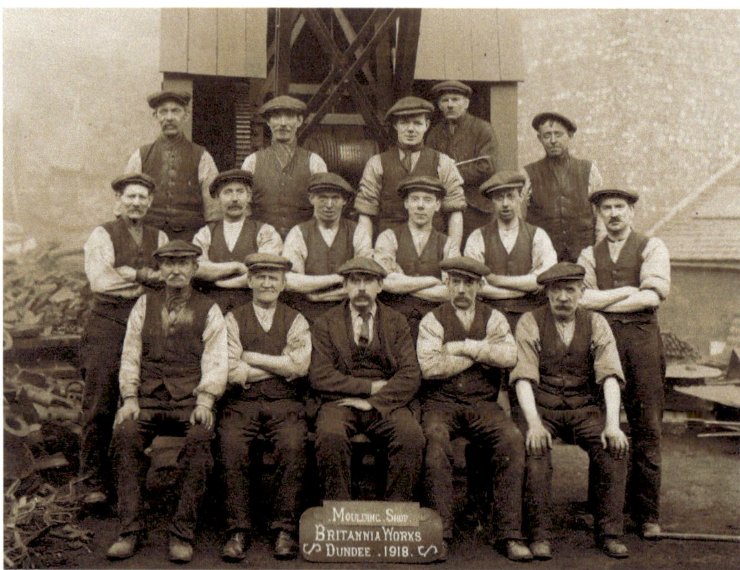

Moulding Shop, Britannia Works, 1918

Britannia Engine and Boiler Works was located in East Dock Street and was occupied from the 1880s by the firm of J. and H. Whyte and Cooper, who made and repaired engines, boilers and other machinery. Given the location, it is not surprising that much of their work involved marine engines. By the time this photograph of the men from the firm's moulding shop was taken, they were Cooper and Greig Limited. The company went into voluntary liquidation in 1926.

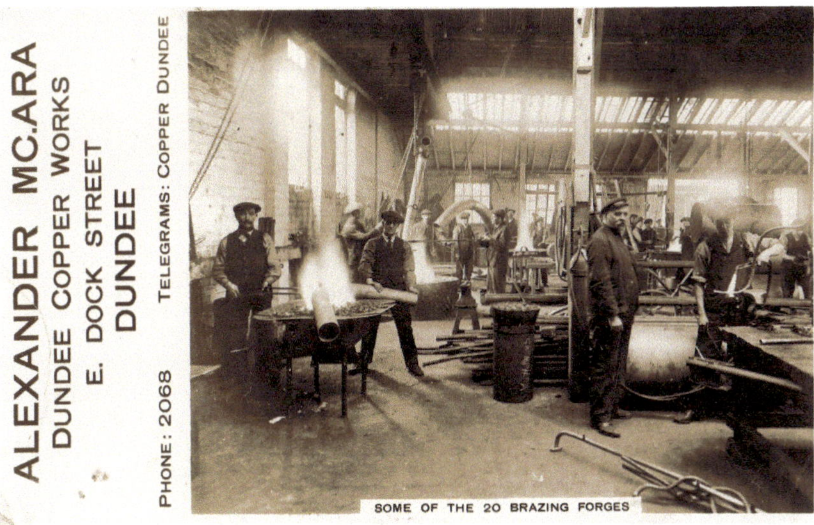

Dundee Copper Works

Alexander McAra's Dundee Copper Works was also situated at East Dock Street. The firm was founded in 1878. The Copper Works supplied several of the fittings for Captain Scott's RRS *Discovery* when it was being built in Dundee at the beginning of the twentieth century. Alexander McAra Jr, son of the company's founder, was one of the city's earliest motoring enthusiasts and was also the proprietor of the West End Garage in Broughty Ferry.

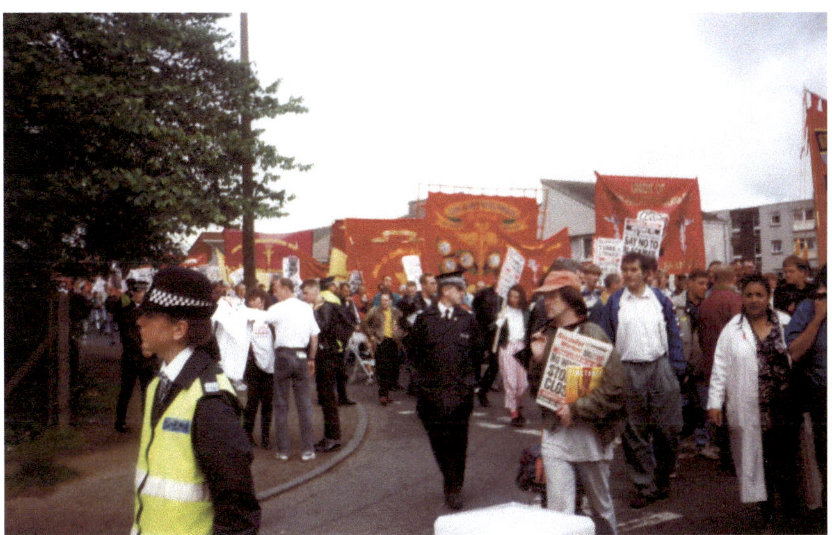

Timex Workers

Timex was one of several manufacturing companies that came to Dundee in the years after the Second World War and provided employment for many in the city as the jute industry underwent its long decline. By 1974 it had 6,000 employees. The company's time in Dundee ended in a bitter dispute in 1993. This photograph shows a demonstration in support of the striking Timex workers passing the factory gates at Harrison Road.

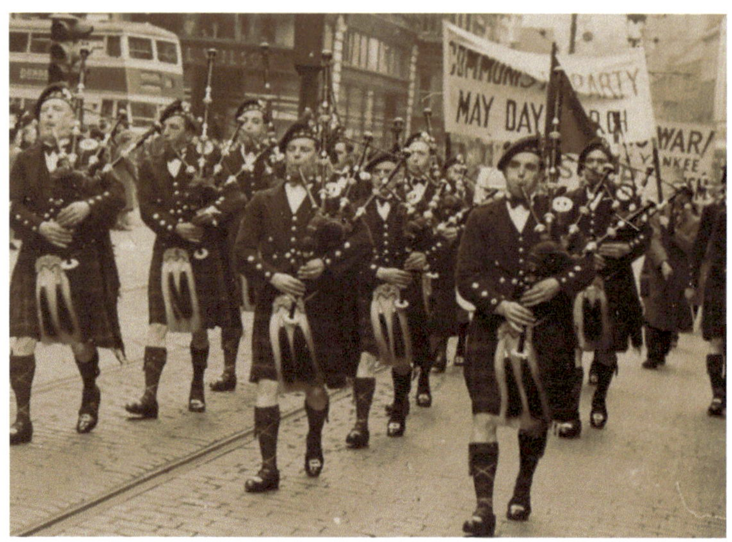

May Day March

The tradition of May Day demonstrations to mark International Workers' Day began in 1889 with a resolution adopted at the Marxist International Workers Congress, which took place in Paris. The date of 1 May was chosen to commemorate a general strike in the United States, which had begun on 1 May 1886. This picture shows a May Day march in the Murraygate in the late 1950s or early 1960s. May Day continues to be marked in the city today.

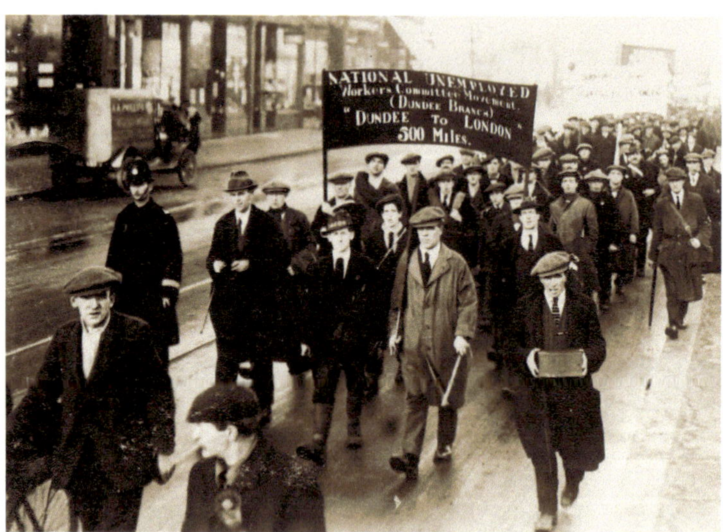

Hunger Marchers

This photograph from January 1923 of a group of unemployed workers on a hunger march does not show Dundee but North Finchley, which was not yet a part of Greater London. It includes a delegation of forty from Dundee who had left home on 29 November 1922 and later joined up with marchers from elsewhere in Scotland. They had hoped to put their case to Prime Minister Andrew Bonar Law but he refused to meet them.

4

Leisure and Sport

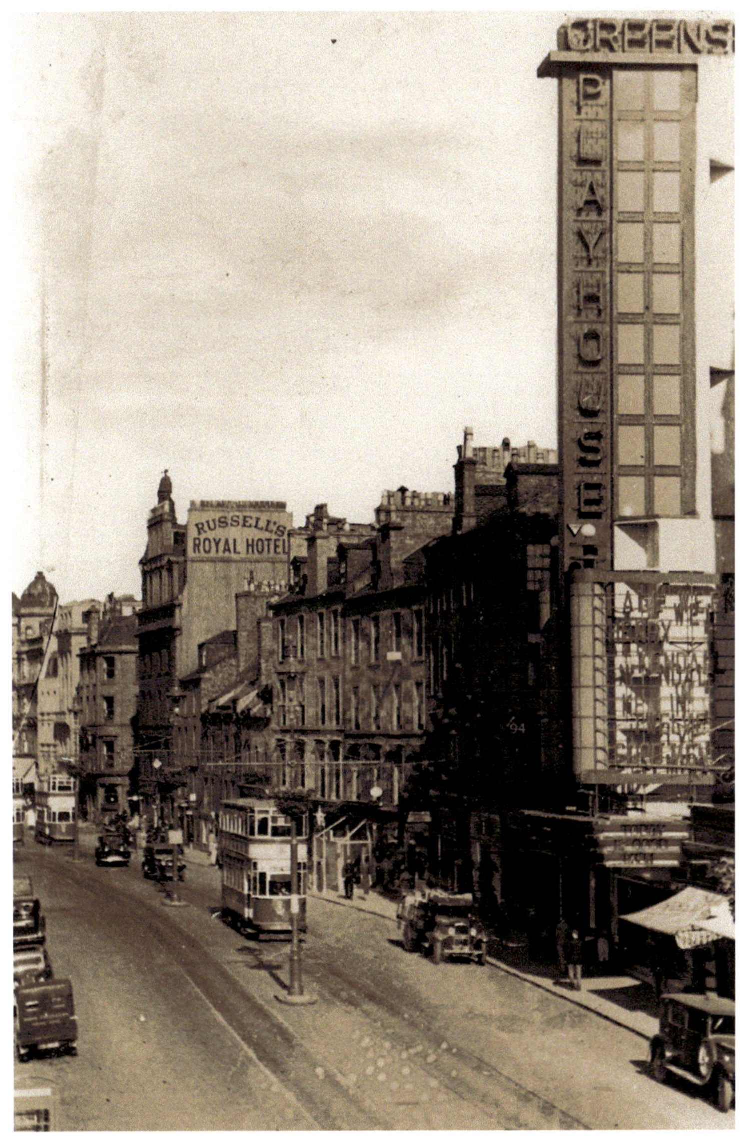

Green's Playhouse.

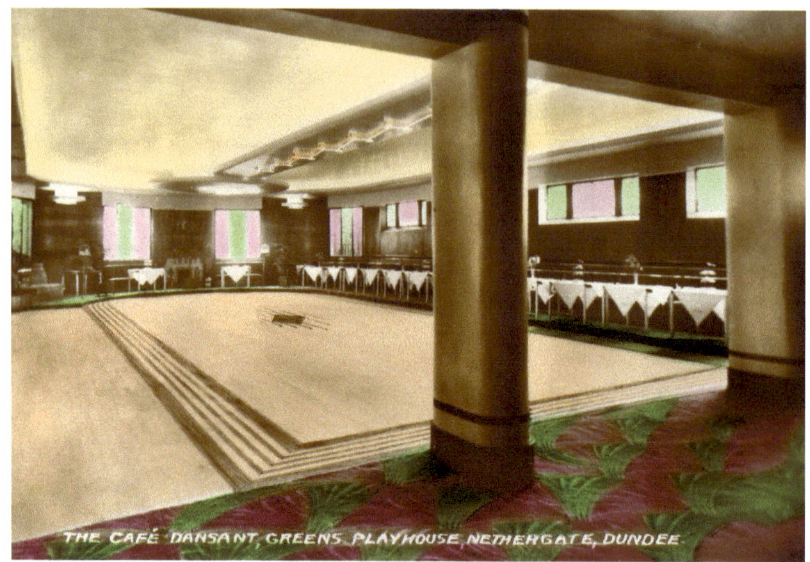

Green's Playhouse Café

Green's Playhouse was one of the largest cinemas in Europe when it opened in 1936. There was seating for more than 2,500 in the stalls and in excess of 1,500 in the balcony and boxes. A 30-ton girder supporting the balcony meant that there were no pillars to obscure views of the 30 feet by 22 feet screen. The facilities also included a 200-seat café, which, with its hard-wood floor, could double as a dance floor, as shown here.

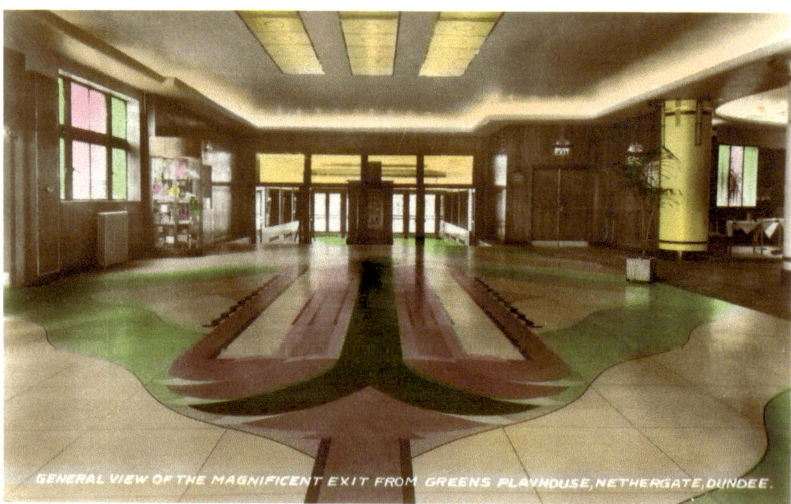

Green's Playhouse Foyer

The décor was luxurious throughout as the vast terrazzo entrance foyer leading to a marble staircase immediately suggested to the visitor. Indeed, the Greens had hoped to replace the Nethergate pavement with an extension of the terrazzo but were refused permission. They were allowed to build the 85-foot-tall steel and glass tower with the cinema's name in neon letters. The letter 'u' sat out of kilter – "We want 'u' in" being the Greens' slogan.

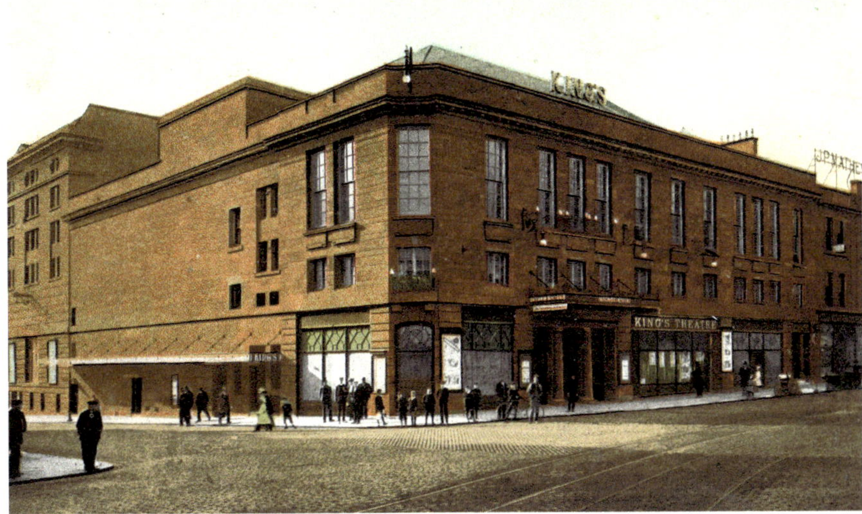

King's Theatre

The King's Theatre and Hippodrome in Dundee's Cowgate, opened in 1909, soon became a regular stop for various touring outfits, from drama and opera companies to music hall and variety acts. Among those who appeared on its stage were Charlie Chaplin and Harry Houdini. It later became a cinema and is still remembered as the Gaumont or the Odeon.

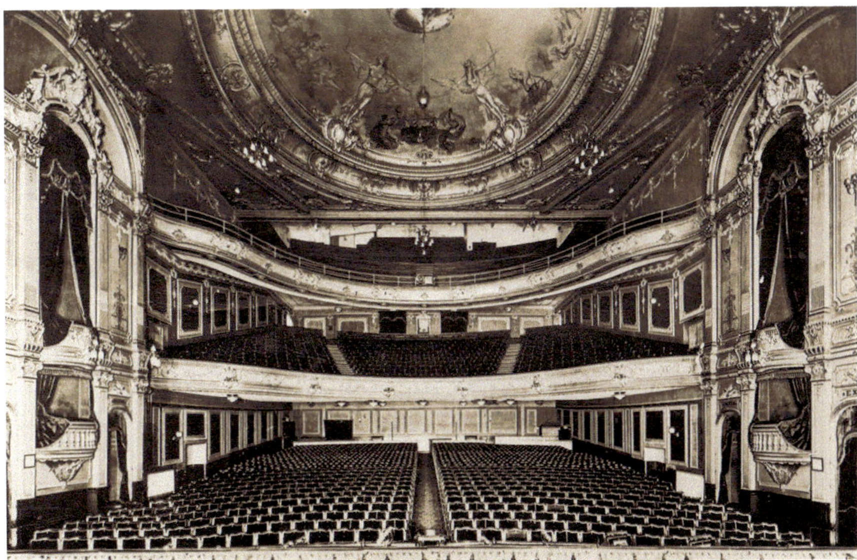

King's Theatre Interior

The interior of the building displayed all the grandeur and spacious opulence of a theatre built during the Edwardian period. The building has been put to various uses over the years since it closed as a cinema, including a bingo hall and a nightclub. Though the interior has been greatly altered, it is thought that many original features survive and there have been many calls for its restoration.

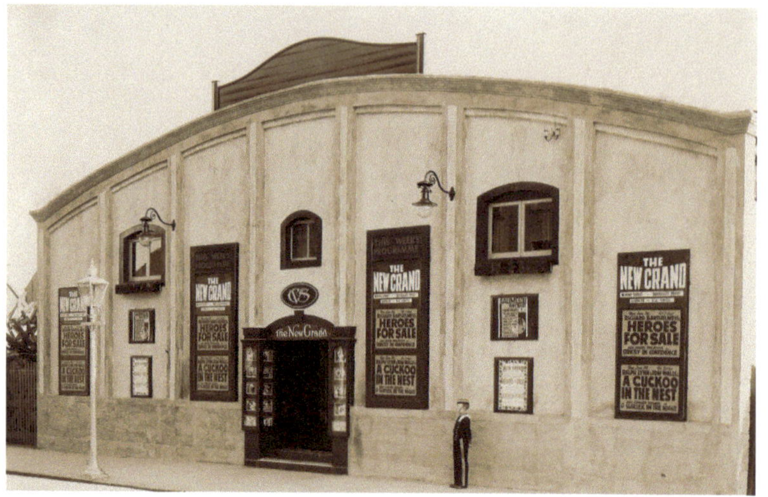

New Grand Cinema

This building in West King Street, Broughty Ferry, opened as The Grand Theatre in 1913. In the 1930s, it became the New Grand Cinema. It is shown here in June 1934 when the main features were 'Heroes for Sale' and 'A Cuckoo in the Nest'. It closed in 1937 and was briefly considered as a possible site for an ice rink. In 1962, the property came into the ownership of the local council and was later demolished.

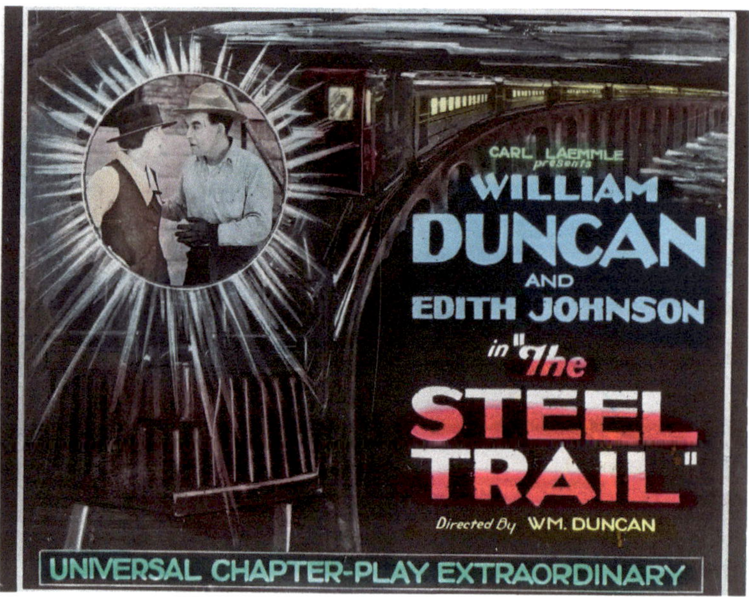

William Duncan

William Duncan was born in Nicolls Lane, Lochee, in 1879. In 1890, his family emigrated to the United States. Duncan made his first silent films as early as 1911 and later began to write and direct. He starred mainly in westerns, specialising in weekly serials such as the one advertised here. His co-star in many of these was Edith Johnson, whom he married in 1921. In the Dundee press his films would be listed as 'starring Dundee's own film star'.

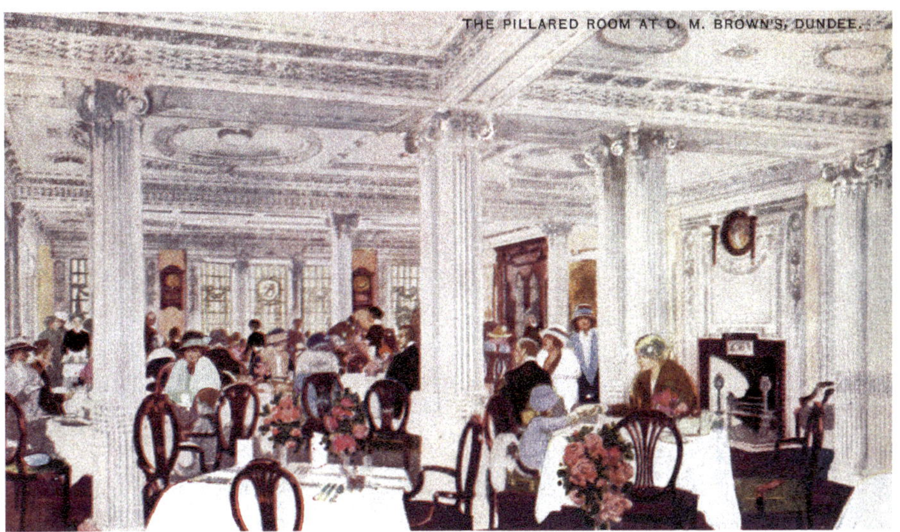

The Pillared Room, D. M. Brown's

Eating out was a different experience in the days before the era of fast food. This is an advertising postcard for the restaurant known as the Pillared Room, which opened in 1910 in D. M. Brown's department store. As well as the pillars that gave the room its name, it boasted a deep pile carpet, fine plasterwork and upholstered chairs. It was the second tearoom in the shop, the other being known as the Panelled Room.

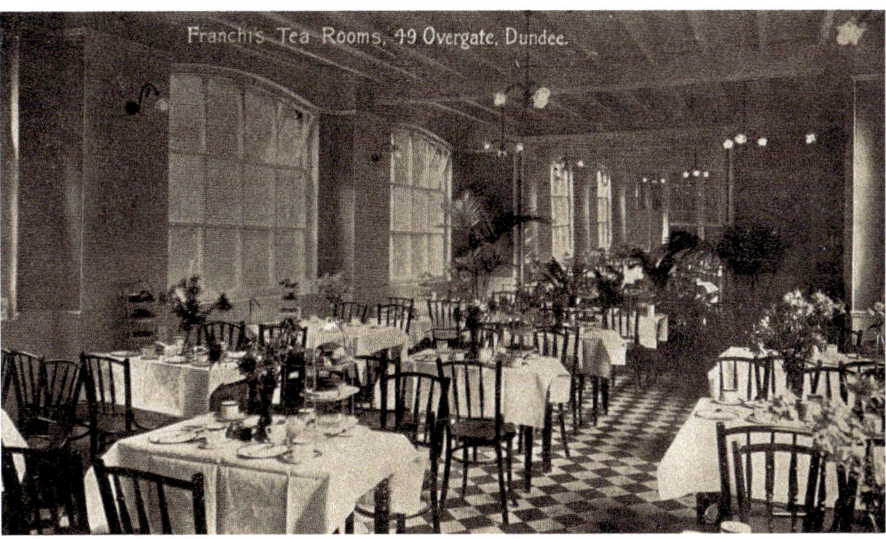

Franchi's

Franchi's was a popular restaurant and tearoom and a major feature of life in the Overgate from the late nineteenth century. The original premises were extended into neighbouring properties, until, by 1929, the restaurant had seating for 200. In 1938, the restaurant became even more of a landmark when a 13-foot neon sign was attached to the front to of the building. Franchi's closed in 1964, due to the impending demolition of the Overgate.

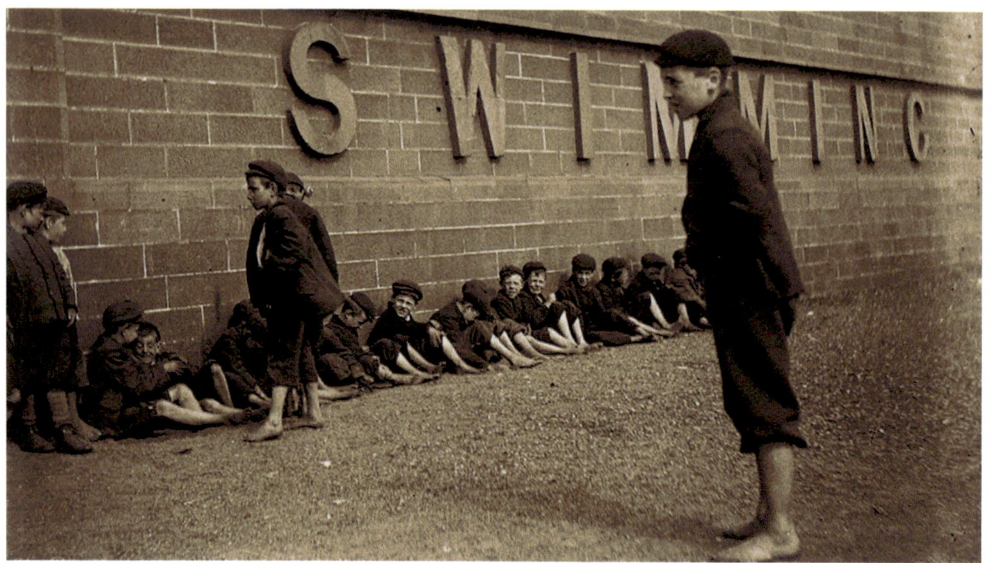

Swimming Baths

Dundee's Swimming Baths were opened at the harbour in November 1873. There were two separate pools each containing around 40,000 gallons of water, which was drawn in from the Tay at high tide by means of a steam pump. The baths were to be Dundee's main swimming facility for the next century and generations of Dundonians would follow in the shoeless footsteps of these young boys.

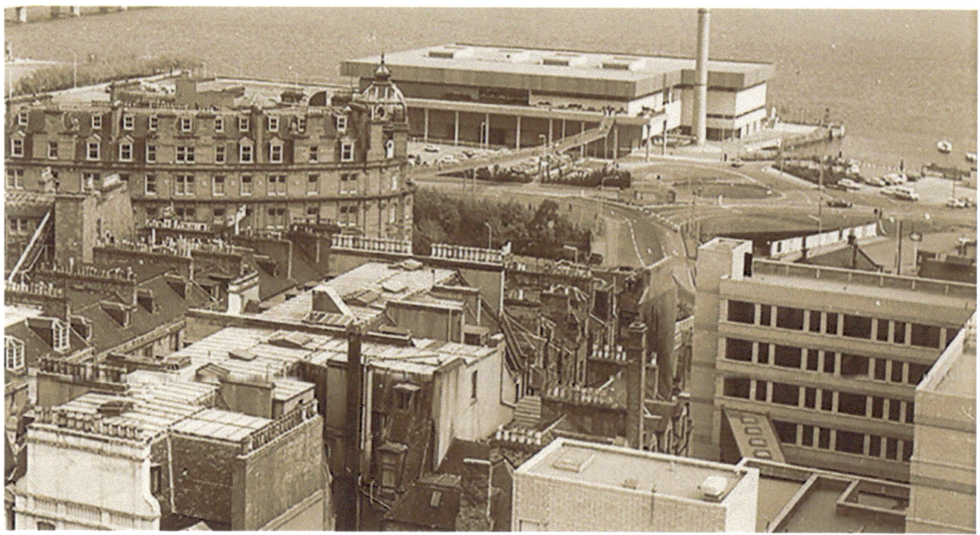

Olympia Swimming Baths

By the early 1970s the old swimming baths were no longer considered sufficient for Dundee's needs. The new Dundee Swimming and Leisure Centre seen here from the Old Steeple, opened in July 1974. It was later modified and renamed as the Olympia. It was ultimately a victim of the plans for the redevelopment of the waterfront. A new Olympia opened at East Whale Lane and the old version was demolished in 2014.

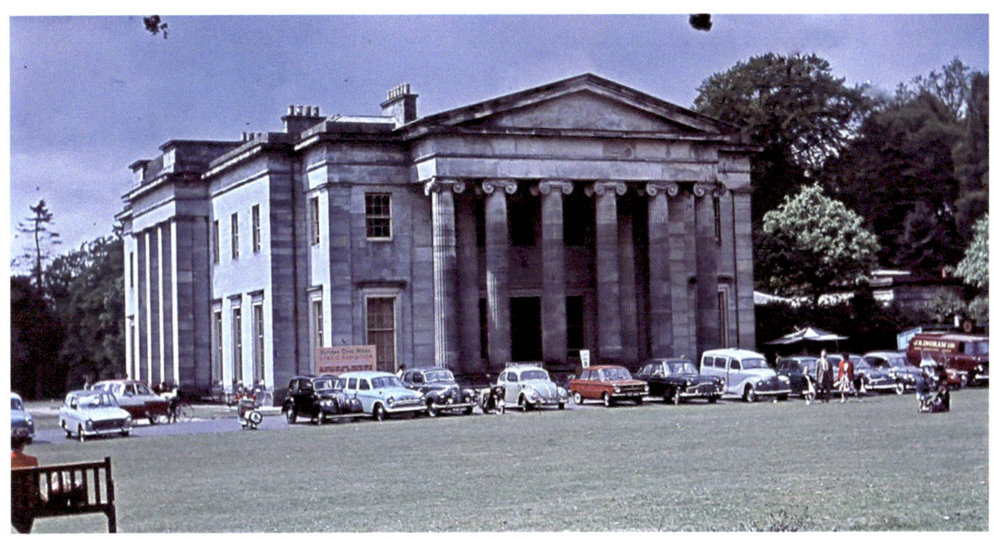

Camperdown Park

The Duncan family's estate was renamed Camperdown in honour of Admiral Duncan's victory against the Dutch at the Battle of Camperdown in 1797. The estate was purchased by the Corporation of Dundee and officially opened as a public park by the then Princess Elizabeth in 1946. Camperdown House dates from the 1820s and is shown here in the 1960s. At this time there was a café in the house and it also housed the clubhouse of the Camperdown Golf Club.

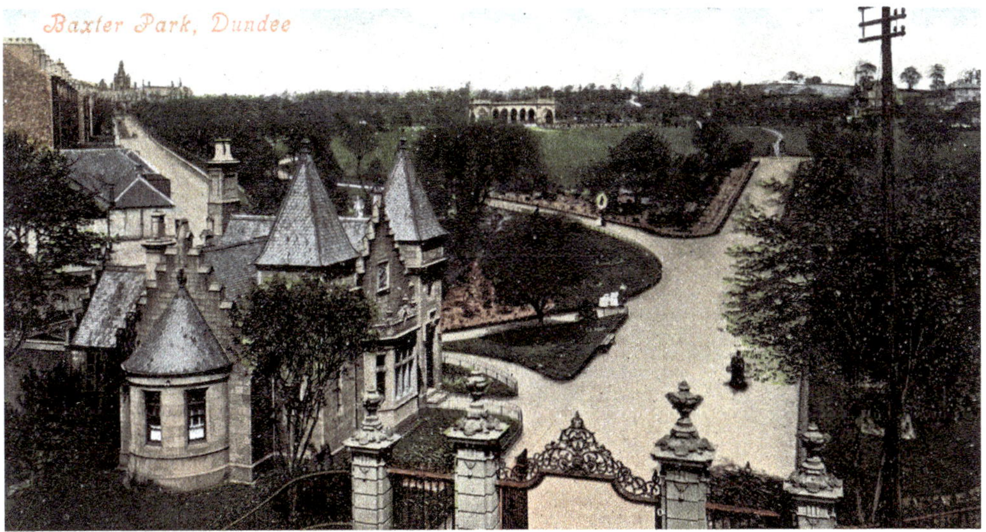

Baxter Park

Linen manufacturer Sir David Baxter and his sisters Mary Ann and Eleanor presented this 37-acre site to the local community for use as a public park. It was designed by Sir Joseph Paxton, the English gardener and architect who designed the Crystal Palace in London. Its centrepiece was the pavilion, seen in the distance here, which was designed by George Henry Stokes. The park was opened on 9 September 1863, in the presence of the Prime Minister, Earl Russell.

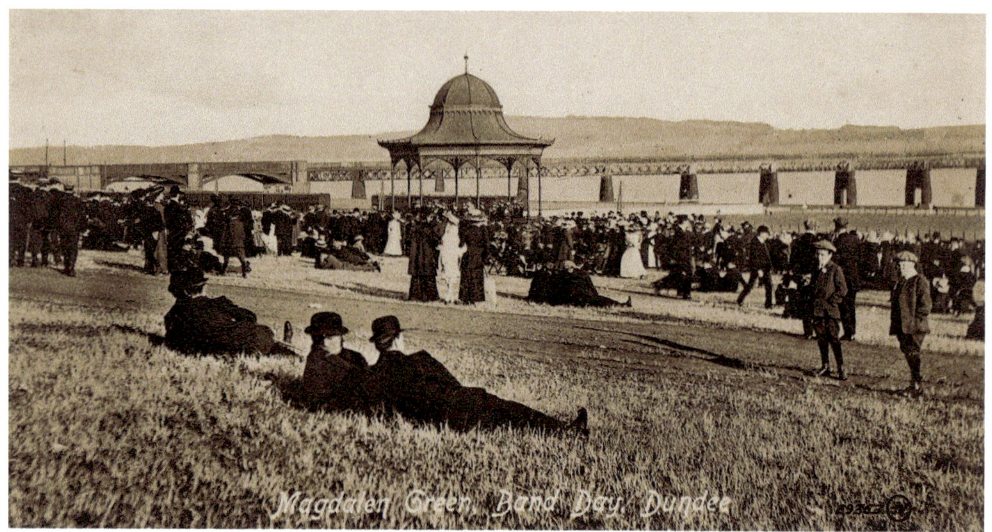

Magdalen Green

Magdalen Yard or Green once extended to the river and provided grazing ground for sheep. The name is said to come from a chapel dedicated to St Mary Magdalen, which used to stand in the vicinity. It is Dundee's oldest public park, notable for its bandstand, which was erected in 1890. More than a century after this photograph was taken, Magdalen Green continues to be enjoyed by the public today, particularly during the annual free festival, WestFest.

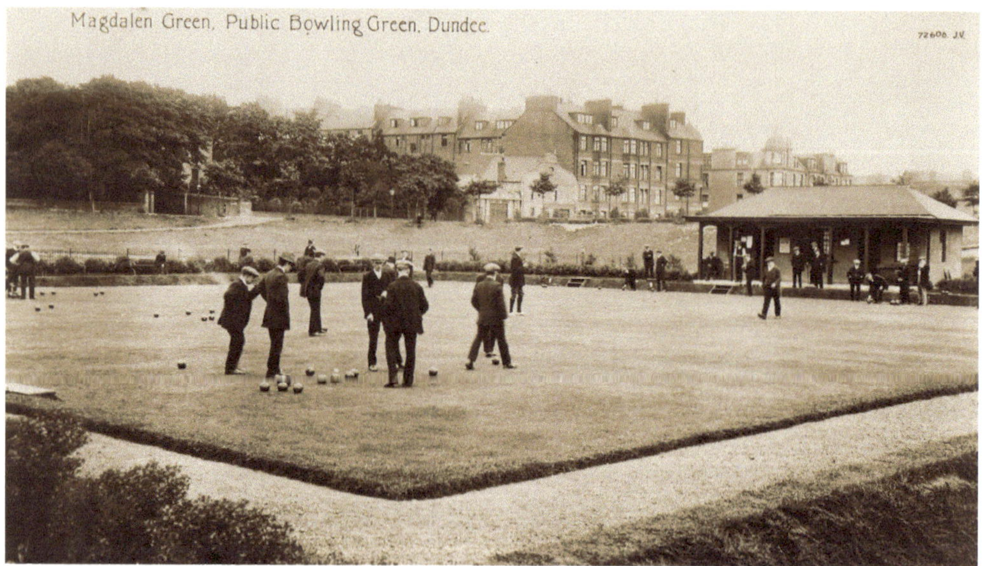

Magdalen Green Public Bowling Green

Bowling has long been a popular sport in Scotland. King James IV is said to have played a variation of the game referred to as 'lang bowlis' at St Andrews in 1469. While several private bowling clubs remain in Dundee, a decline in the sport's popularity and local government cutbacks have meant that public bowling greens like this one at Magdalen Green are rapidly becoming a thing of the past.

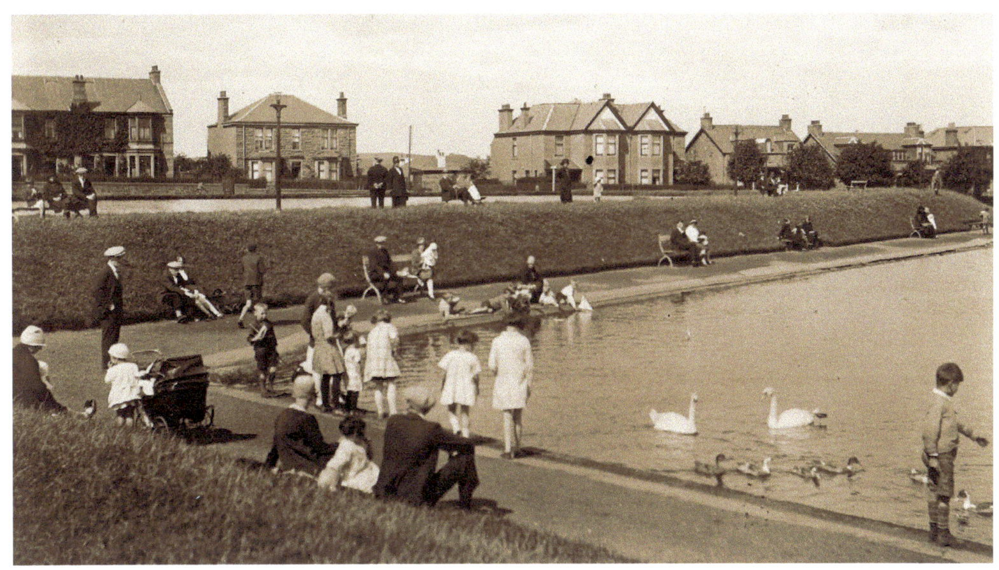

Stobsmuir Ponds

Stobsmuir Ponds date from the mid-nineteenth century and are often known by the local nickname of the 'Swannie Ponds' because of the resident swans, as can be seen in this photograph. There were once as many as four separate ponds but the present configuration of two ponds dates from the early twentieth century. The areas once occupied by the other ponds are now occupied by grassy areas, a play park and a rose garden.

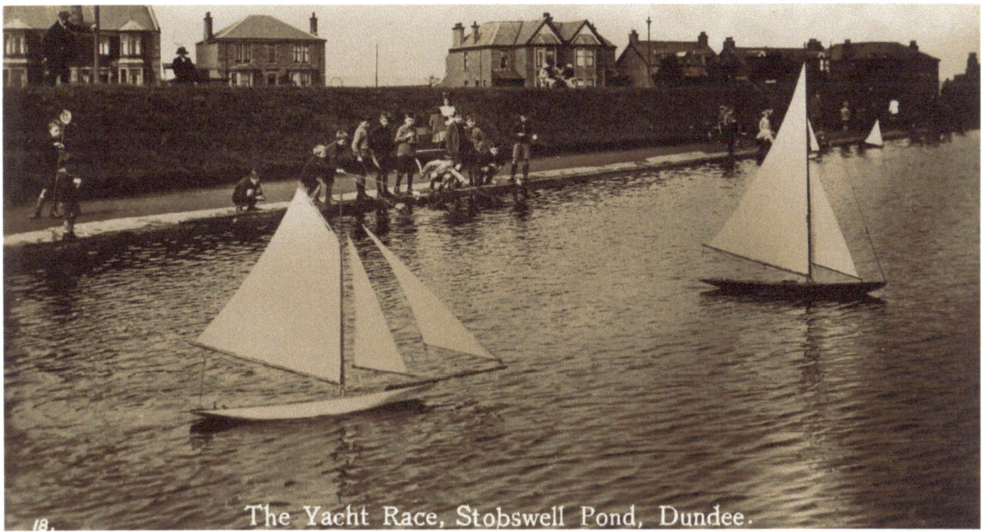

Sailing on the Ponds

The ponds have seen various different activities over the years. These have included fishing and the hire of peddle and rowing boats, as well as the winter activities of curling and skating on the frozen ponds. A consistent activity, as this photograph demonstrates, is the sailing of model boats. The Dundee Model Boat Club was formed in 1885 and has used the ponds ever since.

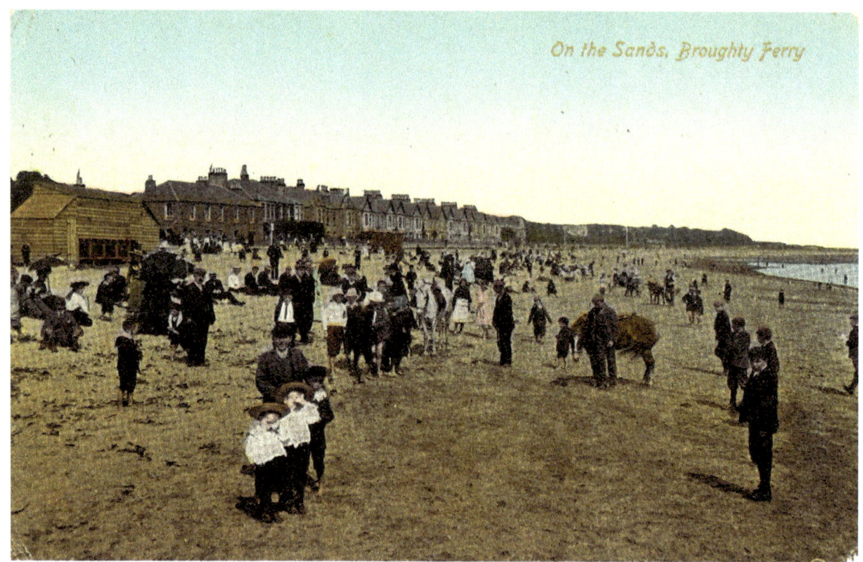

The Sands, Broughty Ferry

In the late nineteenth century, Broughty Ferry began to attract tourists from all over the country, becoming known as the 'Brighton of the North'. Its location, of course, also made it popular with day-trippers from Dundee. This early twentieth-century view would constitute a busy day on the beach today but in the days before widespread car ownership and the increased affordability of foreign travel, it was often far busier.

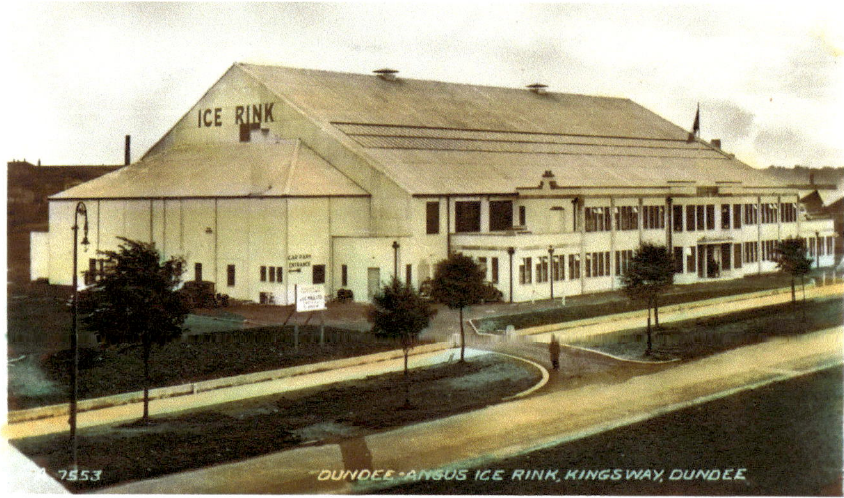

Ice Rink

Dundee Ice Rink was built in 1938 to a design by local architect W. M. Wilson. The skating area itself was 195 feet by 97 feet. It also had a tearoom, a milk bar, lounge and restaurant. As well as providing for local skaters, the rink was home to two successful ice hockey teams – Dundee Tigers and Dundee Rockets. After its demolition and replacement by the Kingsway West Retail Park, a new Ice Arena opened further along the Kingsway.

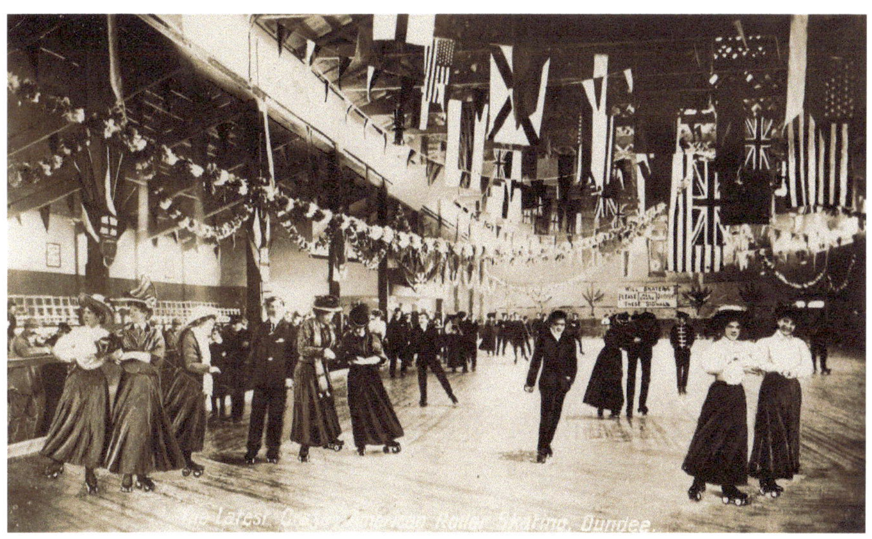

American Roller-skating Rink

The American Roller-skating Rink in Melrose Terrace opened in January 1909. It was said to be the second biggest such rink in the world after one in London. The skating surface was 25,000 square feet and the maple wood floor was imported from America. Roller skating was a craze at this time and by the following year other rinks had opened in the city near Dundee East Station and at Lytton Street off Blackness Avenue.

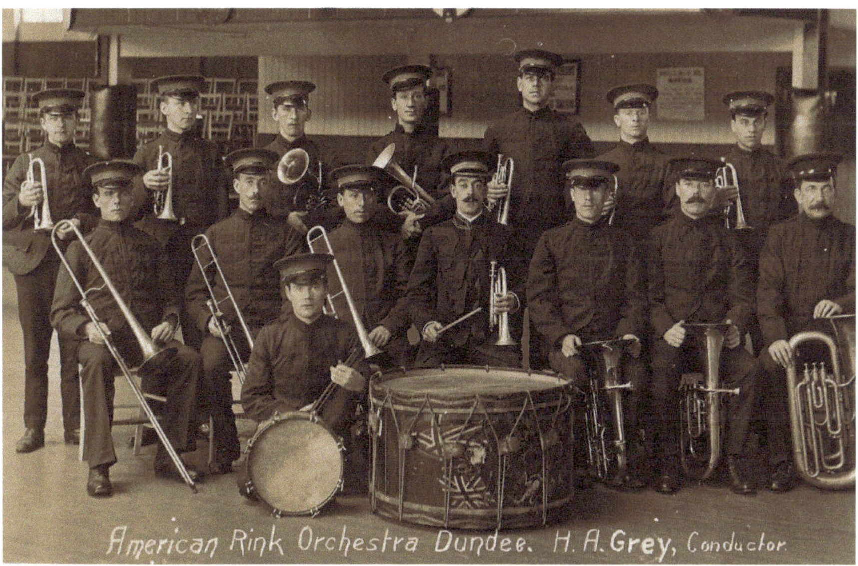

American Roller-skating Rink Band

Roller skaters at the rink would be accompanied by what was referred to as a military band. There were three skating sessions daily and lessons were available for those as yet unfamiliar with the new craze. Like all such fads, the roller-skating craze was short lived. By January 1912, the rink had closed and its contents, including 450 pairs of Samuel Winslow ball bearing roller skates, were put up for auction.

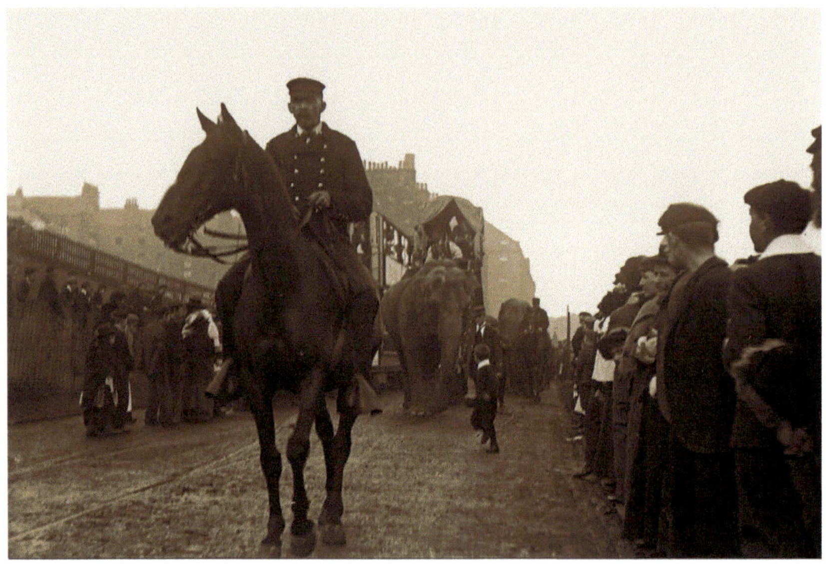

Barnum and Bailey's Circus

Barnum and Bailey's circus – known as the Greatest Show on Earth – visited Dundee in September 1899 boasting a programme of nearly 100 acts. There were also two menageries and what were described as human curiosities. The circus was based at Fairmuir but, as was traditional, paraded through the city on the first day. This photograph shows the parade making its way down Dens Road.

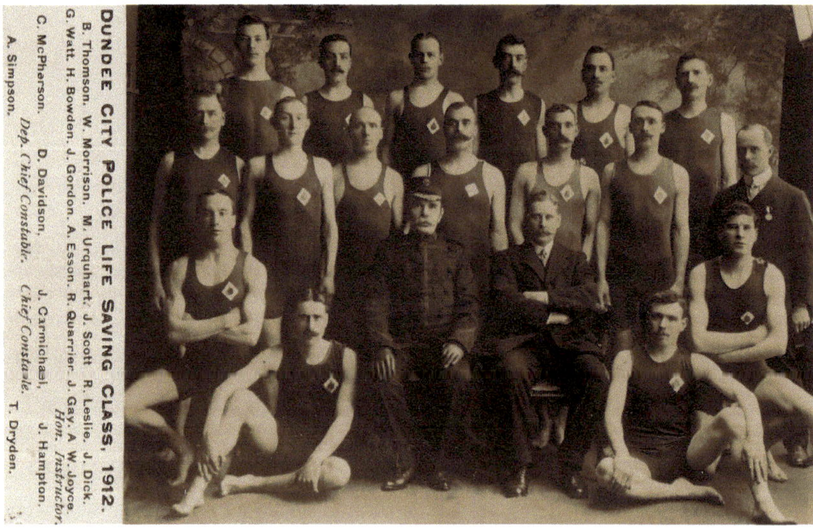

Dundee City Police Life-saving Class, 1912

In the early twentieth century, swimming and life saving were necessary skills for Dundee's police, particularly those who patrolled areas close to the docks or the river. The sixteen officers pictured in swimming costumes here had been learning various methods of life saving for six months and had earned the Royal Life Saving Society's bronze medal. Top of the class was Sergeant Alexnder Esson, who was given a gold medal, with the silver going to Constable James Gordon.

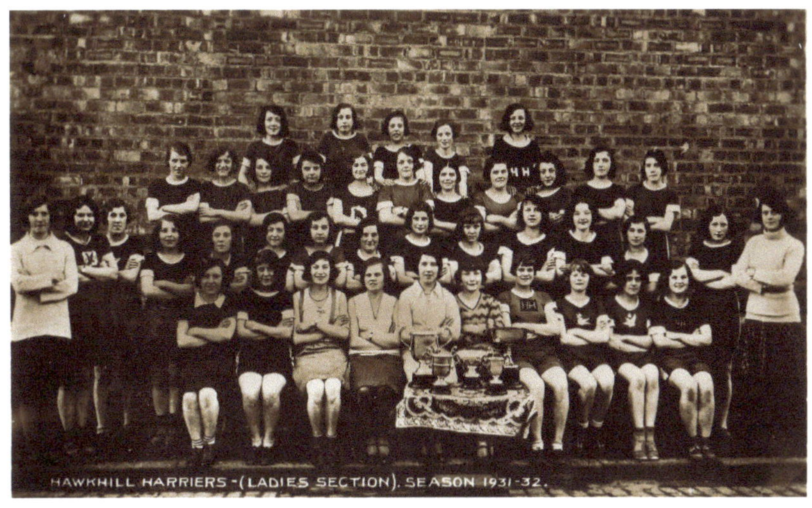

Hawkhill Harriers

Dundee's most famous running club was formed at a meeting on 16 December 1889 and members went for their first run the following night starting from the Hawkhill. The club went into hiatus in the early twentieth century but was re-established in 1924. In 1928, the Harrriers started a ladies' section, the first women's section in any such club in Scotland. The club went on to produce many successful female athletes – among them Liz and Eilish McColgan.

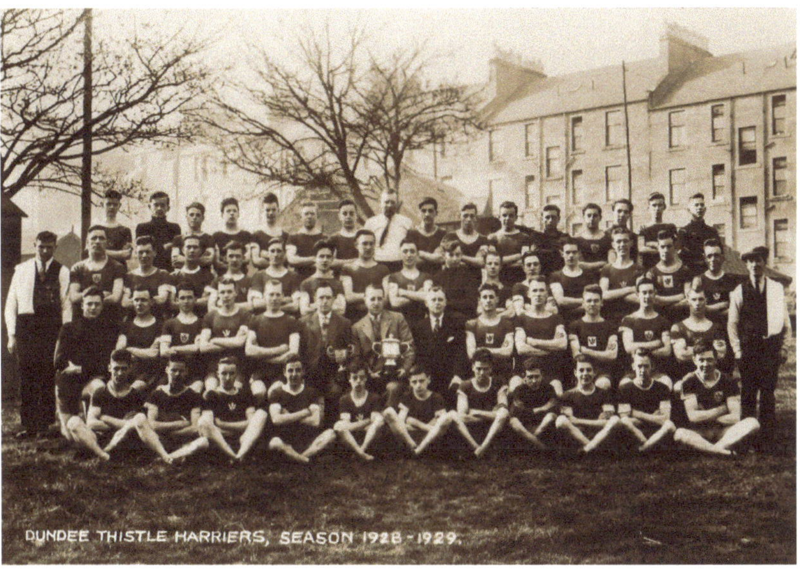

Thistle Harriers

Dundee once had another successful running club, Thistle Harriers, who were also formed in 1889. Among their greatest runners was John Suttie Smith, who competed in the 1928 Olympics. Thistle Harriers' clubrooms were located in the back lands between Seymour Street, Abbotsford Street and Blackness Road. Unfortunately, the rooms were destroyed by a Luftwaffe bomb in 1940. After a wartime merger with Hawkhill Harriers to form Dundee Harriers, Thistle re-emerged but ultimately did not last the pace.

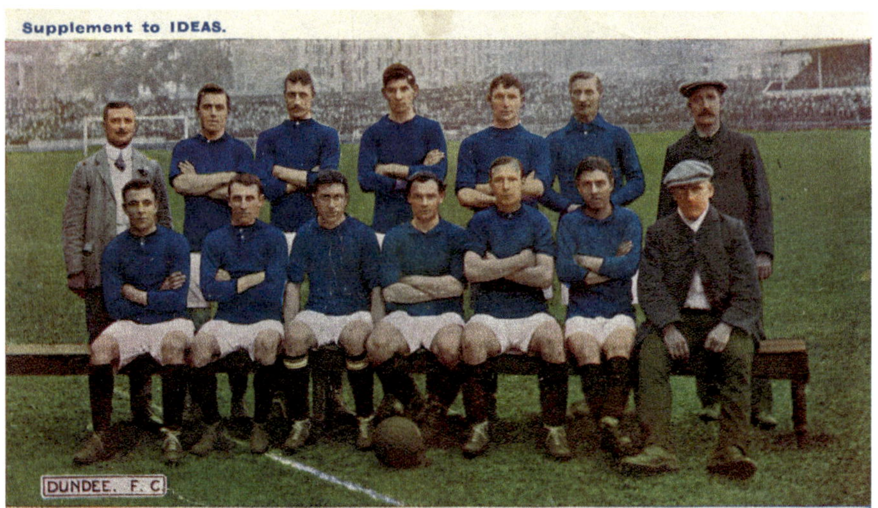

Back Row : W. WALLACE (*Sec. & Manager*), J. CHAPLIN, J. FRASER, A. LEE, B. NEAL, R. CRUMLEY, J. DUNDAS (*Linesman*),
Front Row : J. BELLAMY, G. LANGLANDS, A. MACFARLANE, H. DAINTY, A. MENZIES, J. LAWSON, W. LONGAIR (*Trainer*).

Dundee FC

Dundee Football Club was founded in 1893 following a merger between two local clubs – East End and Our Boys. This postcard, issued as a supplement to *Ideas* magazine, is almost certainly the first image of the team that was issued in colour. It depicts the team around the time of their 1910 Scottish Cup victory. Dundee beat Clyde 2-0 in a second replay of the final after drawing 2-2 and 0-0.

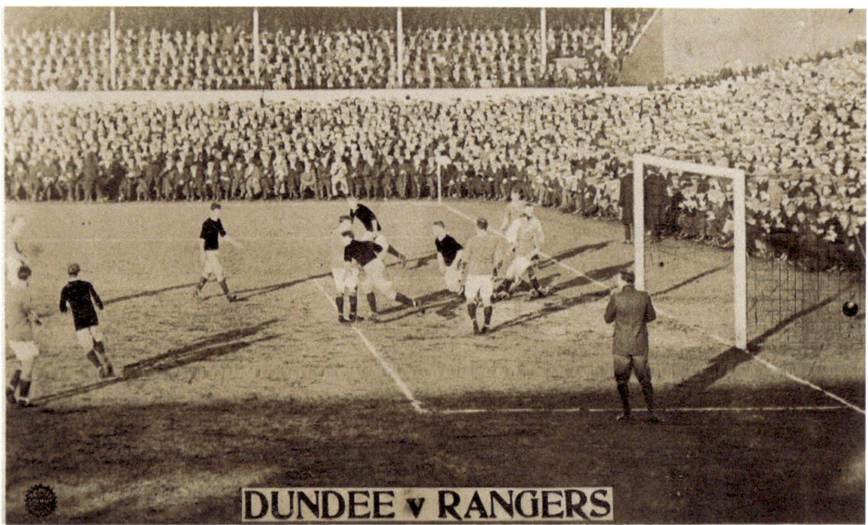

Dundee vs Rangers

This match photograph shows Dundee vs Rangers in the Scottish Cup third round at Dens Park on 25 February 1911 before a record crowd (at the time) of 30,000. It shows former Rangers player Robert Hamilton scoring the first goal in a match that Dundee eventually won 2-1. This image was sold by chemist A. H. Ross of Strathmartine Road as a postcard and also as a larger print. Dundee went on to lose to Hamilton Academicals in the semi-final.

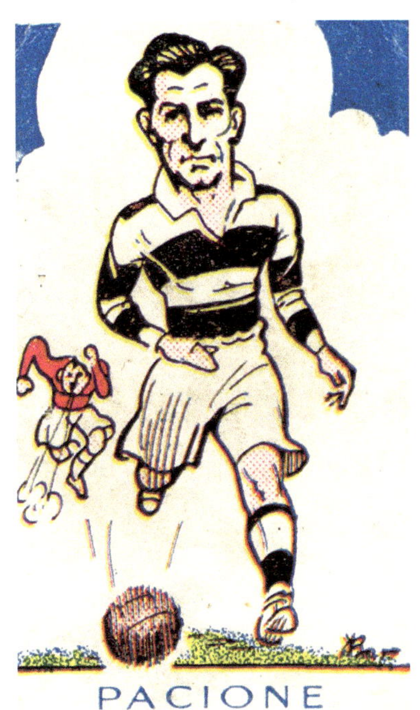

Emilio Pacione

This cigarette card of a Dundee United player features Emilio Pacione, who played as a centre forward and winger for the club between 1945 and 1950. His brother Sidney played left back for Aberdeen and Hibernian. Both brothers had played for Lochee Harp. Sid later became assistant rector of St John's High School, while Emilio worked in Timex and NCR. Sid died in 2009 and Emilio in 2012 at the age of ninety-two.

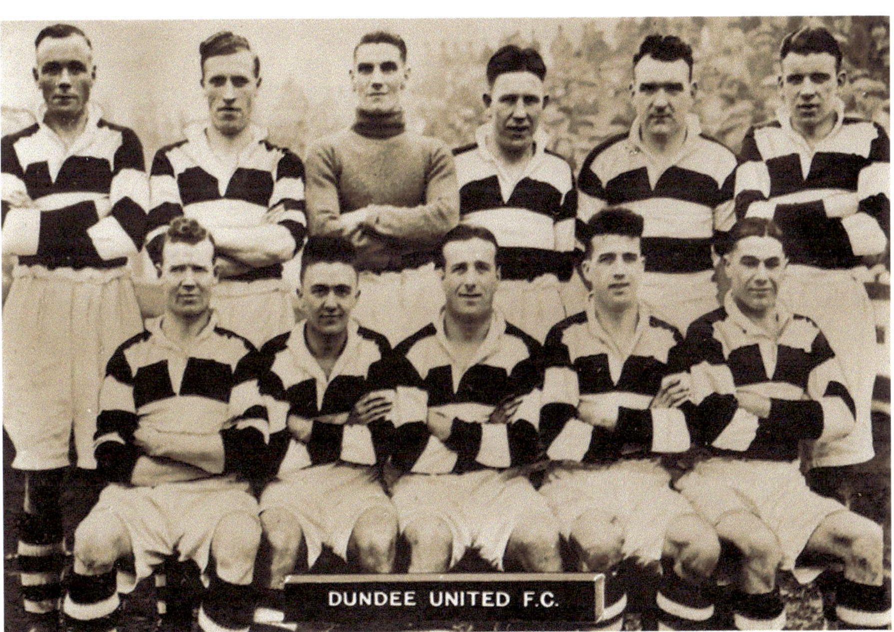

Dundee United

Dundee United was formed as Dundee Hibernian in 1909 and took the name Dundee United in 1923. This team photo dates from the 1930s. Even though it is not in colour, it is instantly apparent that Dundee United are not wearing their now familiar strip. United's official team colours were black and white until 1969 when they adopted the tangerine and black strip.

5

Transport

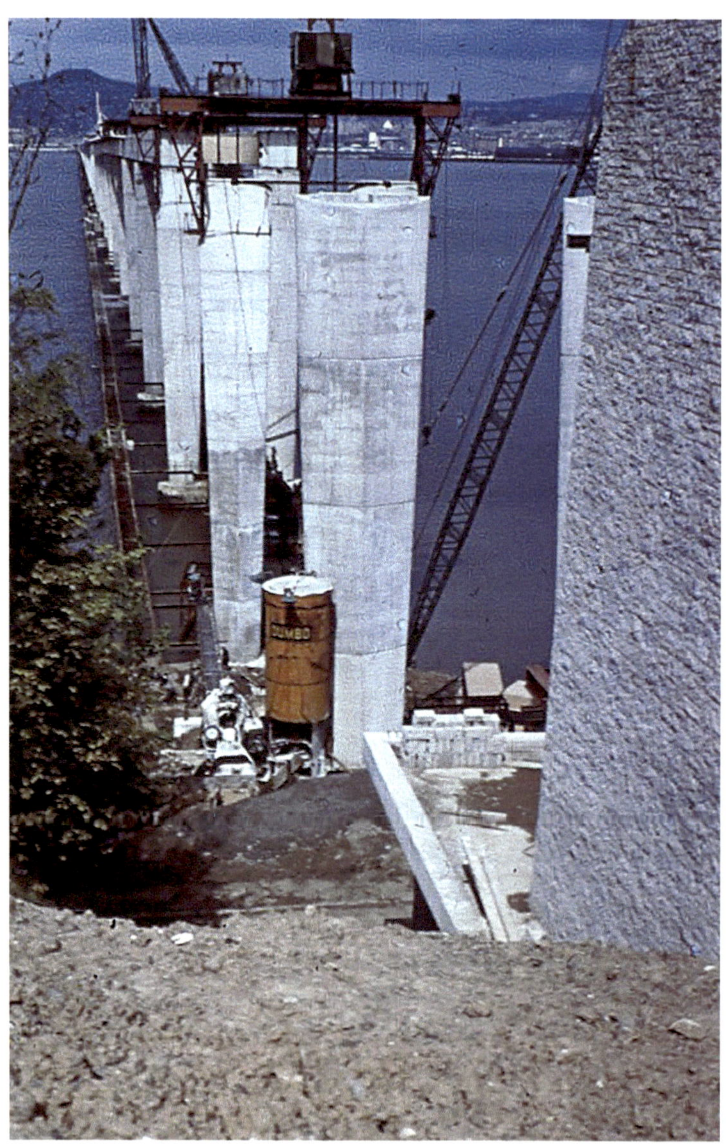

The Tay Road Bridge under construction.

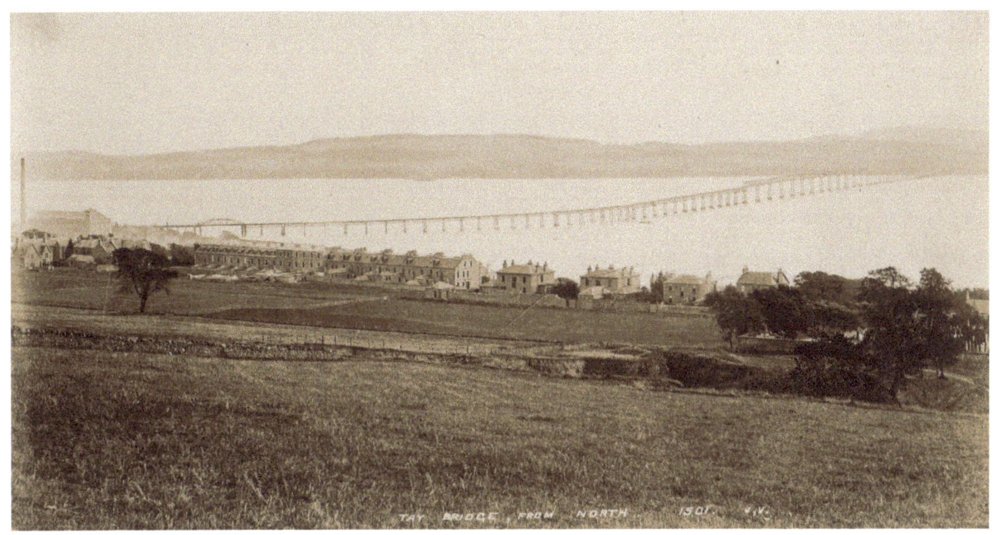

Tay Bridge

Designed by engineer Thomas Bouch, the original Tay Bridge opened in June 1878 and was regarded as a triumph of Victorian engineering. Bouch was knighted in June 1879 by Queen Victoria. Tragically, the bridge collapsed during a ferocious storm on the night of 28 December 1879 with the loss of all the passengers and crew of a train that was crossing at the time. Bouch's reputation never recovered and he died less than a year later.

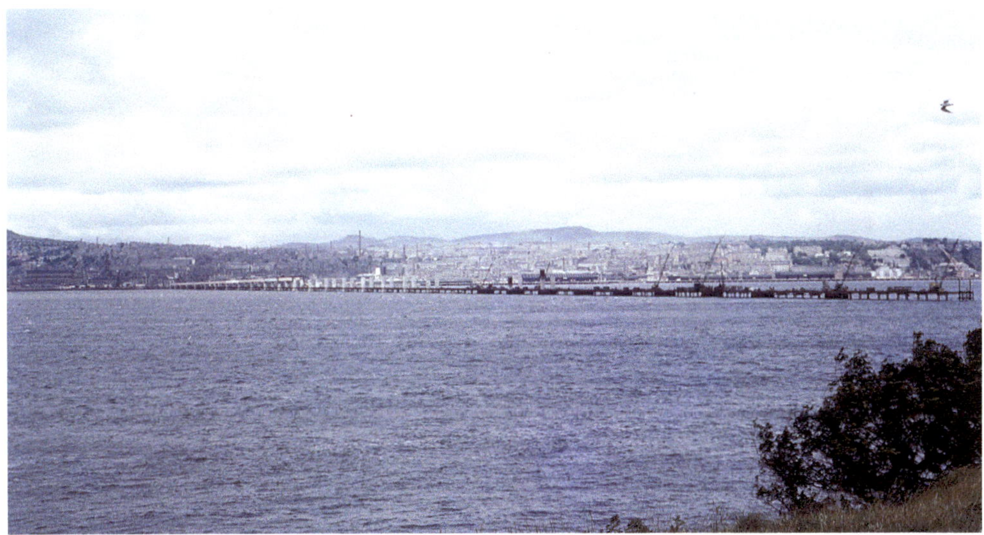

The Tay Road Bridge

The Tay Road Bridge is 1.4 miles long and stretches between Dundee and Newport-on-Tay. It is shown here during its construction. The bridge was designed by William A. Fairhurst and was built between 1963 and 1966. Tragically, five workers died during the construction of the bridge and William Logan, managing director of the main building contractor Duncan Logan Limited and founder of Loganair, died in a plane crash in January 1966.

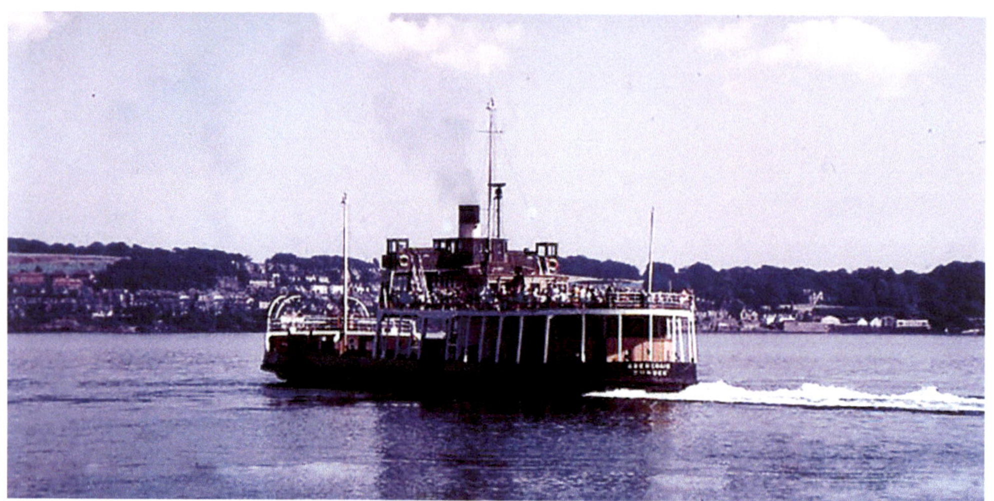

Abercraig

For centuries, the only way to cross the Tay at Dundee was by boat, but it was only following a disaster in 1815 when eighteen people died that the service began to be regulated. A scheduled ferry service began in 1821. This image shows the *Abercraig*, one of the Fifies (as the ferry boats were known locally). It was taken on 18 August 1966 – the last day of the ferry service and the day that the Tay Road Bridge opened.

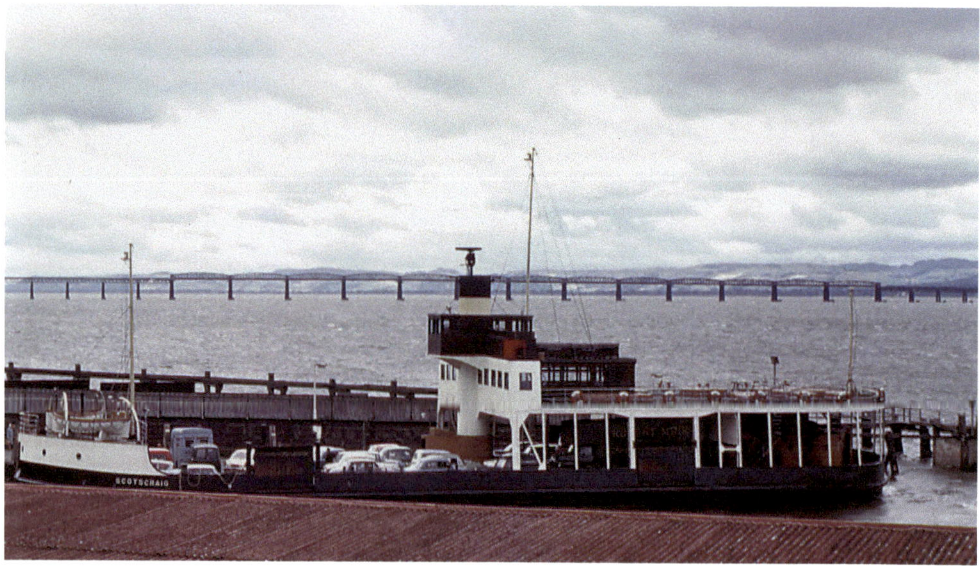

Scotscraig

This picture shows the *Abercraig's* sister vessel the *Scotscraig* at Newport-on-Tay, the destination of the ferries on the Fife side. After the road bridge opened, the *Scotscraig* and *Abercraig* were sold to Malta. The *Abercraig* was eventually scrapped but in 1980 *Scotscraig* went on to be used in the production of the film *Popeye*, which starred Robin Williams. It later sank while being towed to a new location and is now a popular wreck attraction for divers.

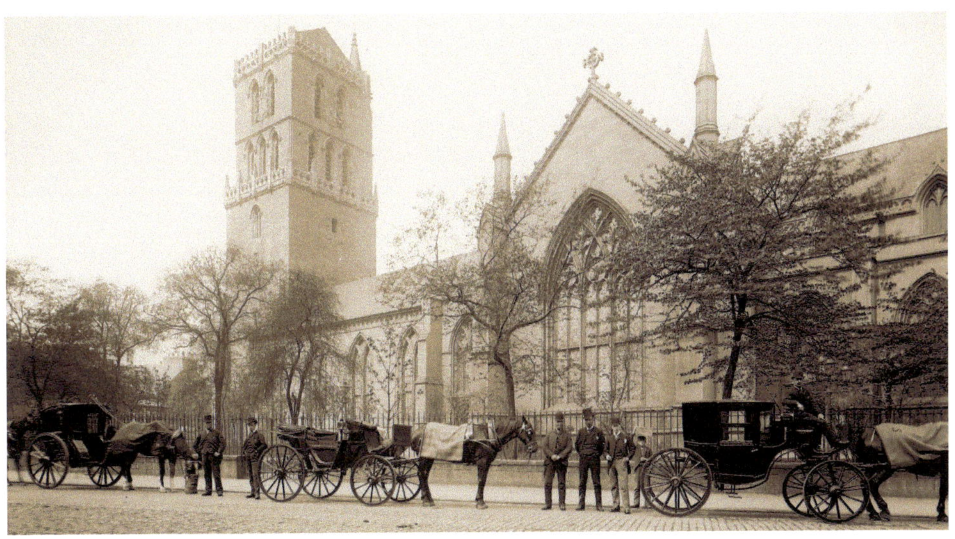

Cab Stance, City Churches

There has been a cab stance outside the City Churches since Victorian times. At this time the cabs were, of course, horse drawn. On the left is the two-wheel hansom cab as patented by Joseph Hansom in 1834. In the middle is a two-person landaulet, a cut down version of the four-person landau with its collapsable roof. Finally, there is a Clarence, commonly known as a 'growler' because of the sound this type of cab made on the cobbled streets.

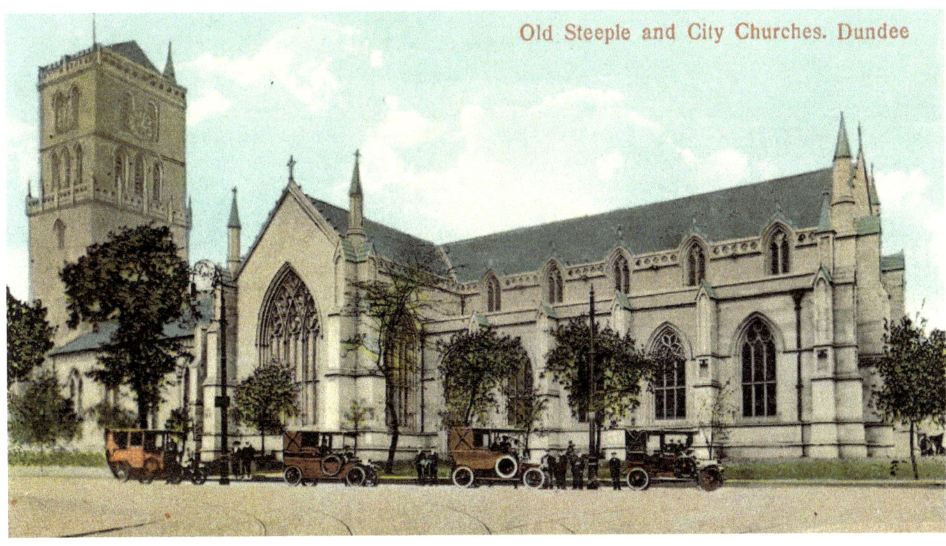

Motor Taxis

The introduction of the motor car marked the slow death of horse-drawn transport in Dundee and elsewhere. Car registration was introduced in 1904, with the first Dundee registration, TS1, going to photographer Alexander Watt. This registration was later passed to the city for use on the Lord Provost's car. The motorisation of taxis happened fairly quickly. There were forty-one motor taxi licences issued before the First World War and by 1920 there were almost a hundred.

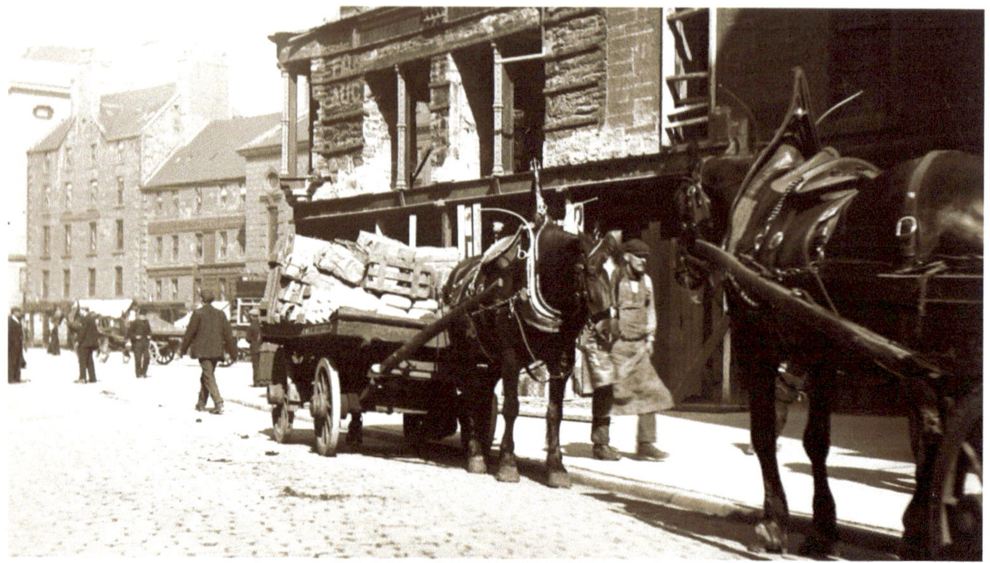

Horse Transport at the Overgate

The start of the Overgate at its junction with the High Street is shown here at the beginning of the twentieth century. Horses would have been a very common sight on Dundee's streets at the time and were the main means of transport for delivery. This had been the case for centuries, but would begin to change within a few years, though Dundee's last workhorse, Paddy, and his carter, Chic Donaldson, could still be seen in the 1970s.

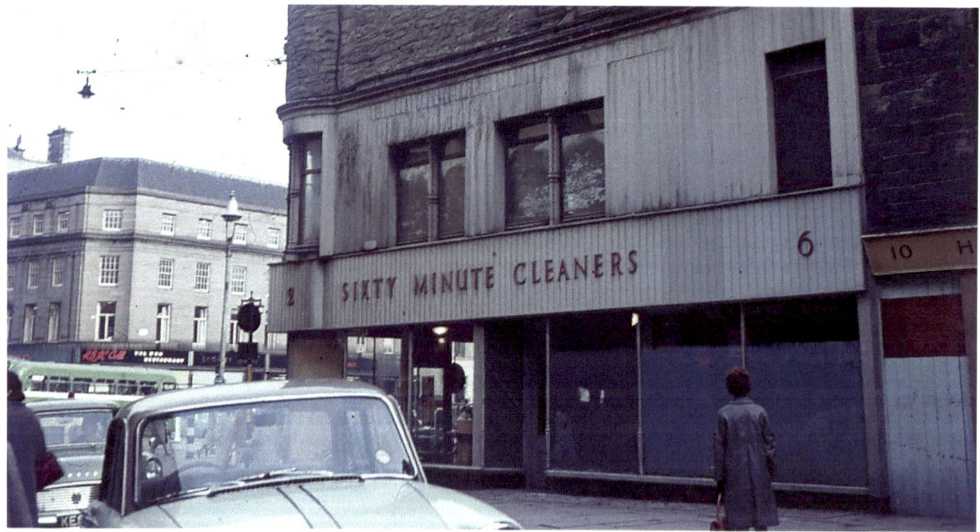

Motor Transport at the Overgate

Moving on around sixty years, this is another view of the same spot in the last days of the old Overgate. The car has definitely taken over, squeezing into the narrow street that was clearly never designed for motor transport. Catering for the growth in the number of cars was a major factor in the changes that took place in Dundee of the 1960s, arguably to the detriment of much else.

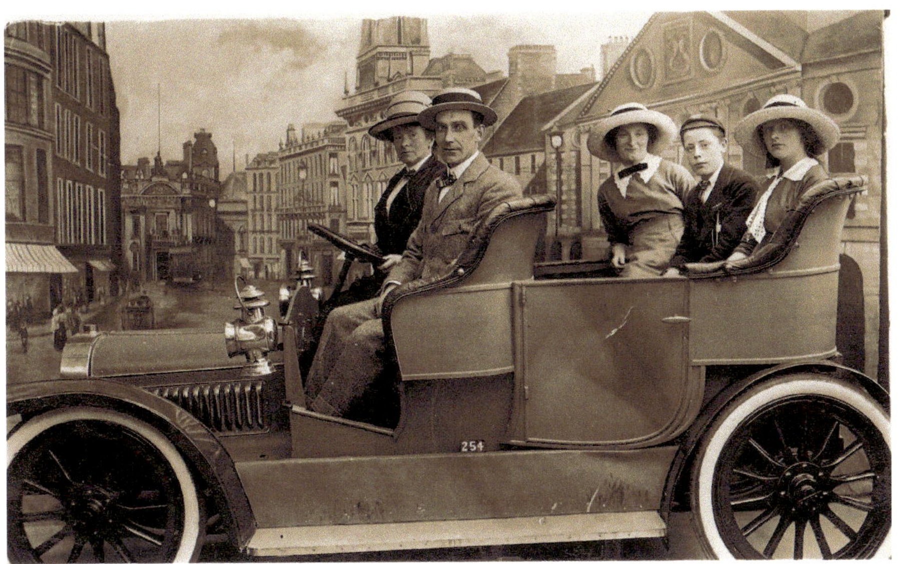

Car Ride

These people are not travelling anywhere in this motor car, which is probably just as well because they are all looking at the photographer, rather than the road. The car is being used a prop by photographer D. G. Brown, and the backdrop is a representation of Dundee High Street. Brown would set up a studio at the Promenade in Broughty Ferry in summer to capture images of holidaymakers from around 1910.

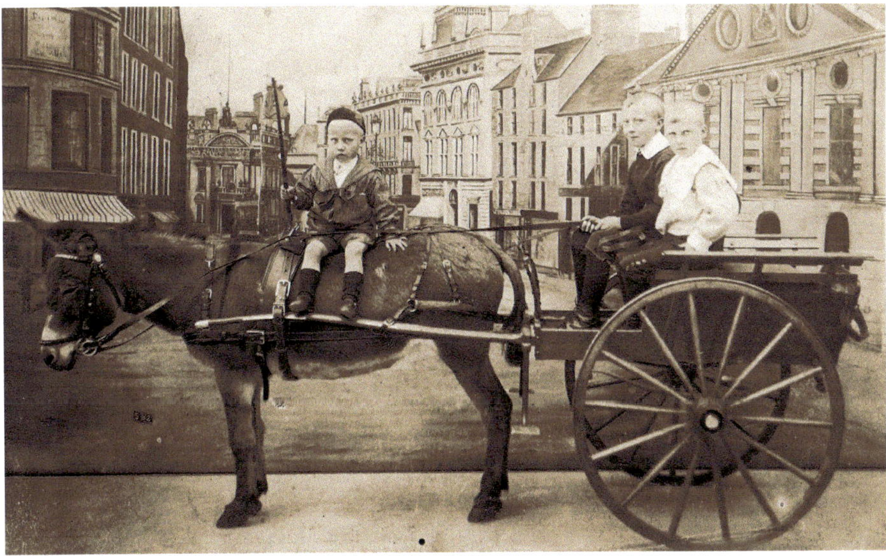

Cart Ride

The backdrop clearly predates motor transport and here it is being used from when a photographer called Philip E. Low operated from the Broughty Ferry Promenade. The set-up with the cart or motor car was one of two regularly used at the temporary studio. The other one used a rowing boat that the subjects would sit in to accompany a backdrop of Brought Ferry Harbour showing the castle.

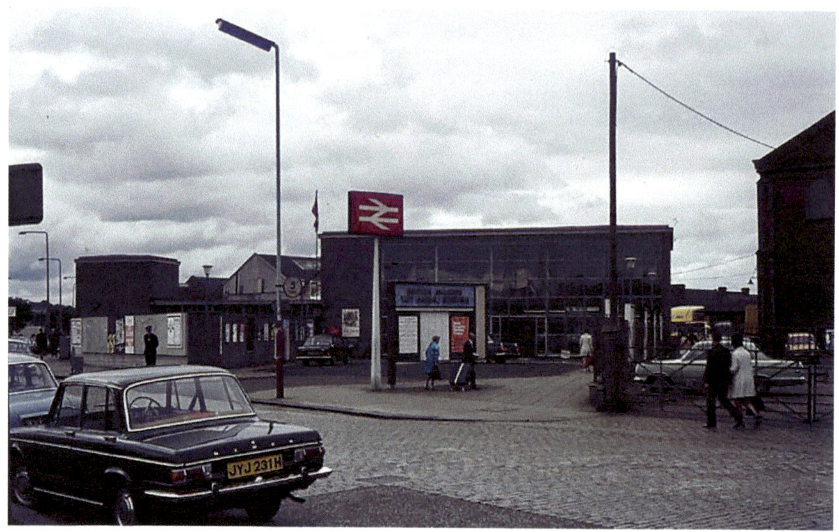

Dundee Railway Station

Dundee railway station was originally known as Dundee Tay Bridge station, and, as the name suggests, was built in connection with the railway crossing across the Tay. It was opened in 1878 by the North British Railway Company and was once one of three city centre railway stations, each run by a different railway company. This image shows the station entrance as it looked in the early 1970s.

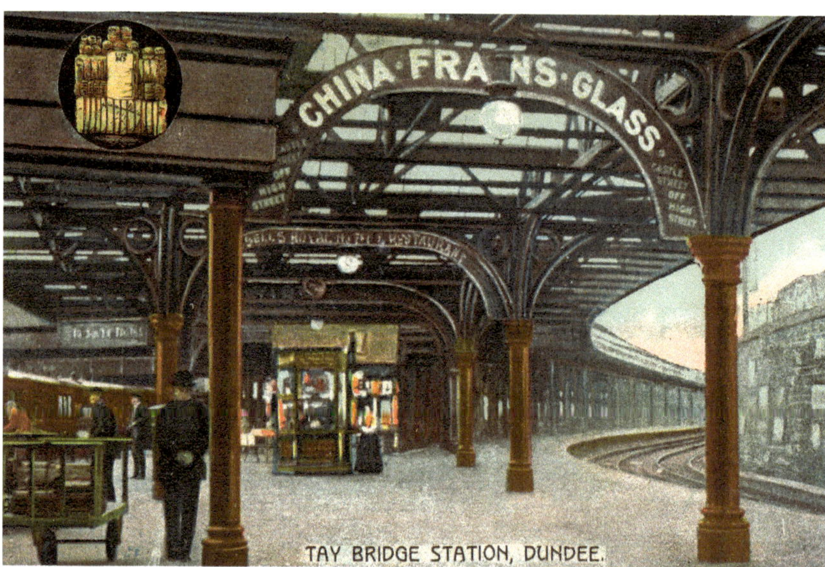

Tay Bridge Station Platform

This is an old postcard of the interior of Tay Bridge station at platform level. This view remains recognisable today, though the central area here is now enclosed and entered via ticket barrier. The two outer platforms visible here (numbers one and four) can accommodate through trains and the two central platforms (numbers two and three) are for trains starting or ending their journeys at Dundee. It was 1928, however, before platform numbers were introduced at the station.

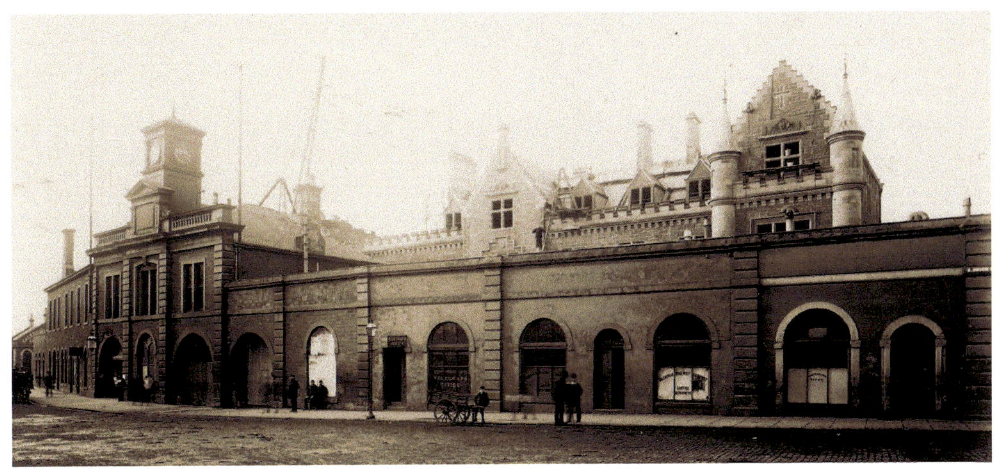

Dundee West Station

Dundee West station was situated in South Union Street. It was originally opened in 1847 for the Dundee & Perth Railway. This image shows the later version of the station that was built in 1865, with the third and final version being built behind it. This dates the photograph to 1889–90 when the new station was built to a design by Thomas Barr for the Caledonian Railway Company.

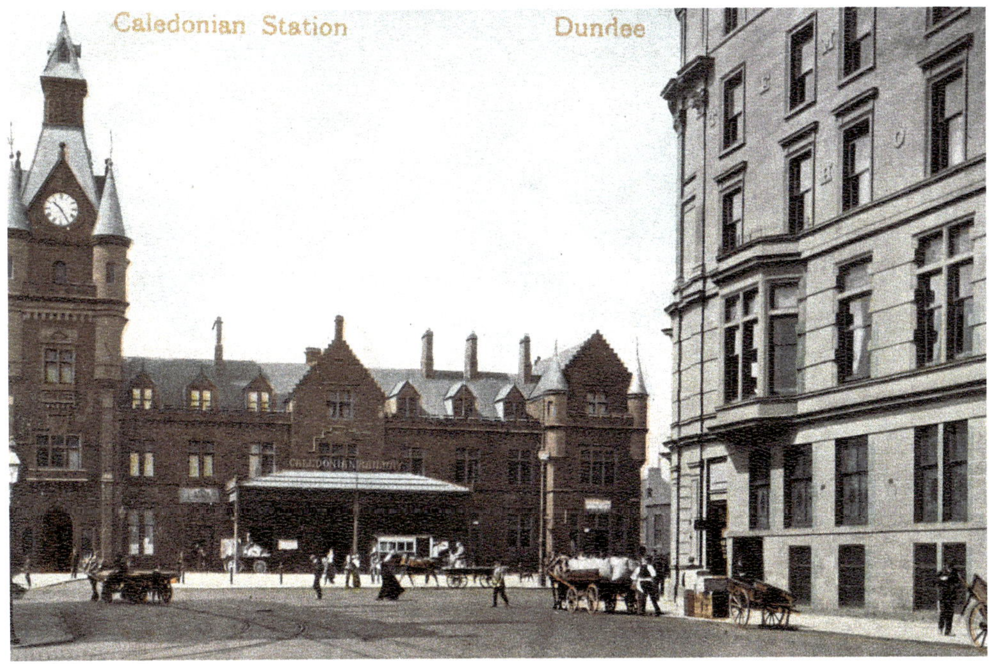

Dundee West Station

This old postcard gives a better idea of the location of Dundee West station with reference to what is currently the Malmaison Hotel, whose Dock Street side is shown to the right of the image. The station stood for around seventy-five years, closing to both passengers and goods traffic in 1965. It was demolished and soon after the site became part of the network of roads leading to the Tay Road Bridge.

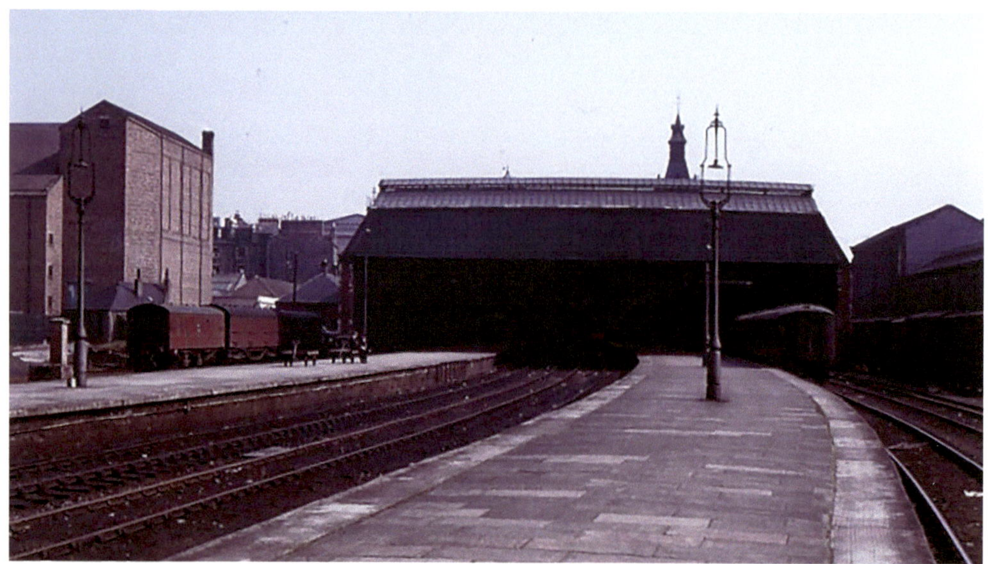

Dundee West Station Platform View

A view of the platforms at Dundee West station looking east, back in the direction of South Union Street. The spire of the station's clock tower can be seen above the platform roof. The red-brick building on the west of the image is the back of the Green's Playhouse. The Victorian lampposts date from the time of the 1890 rebuild when the station's platforms were lit with gas for the first time, having previously been illuminated by oil lamps.

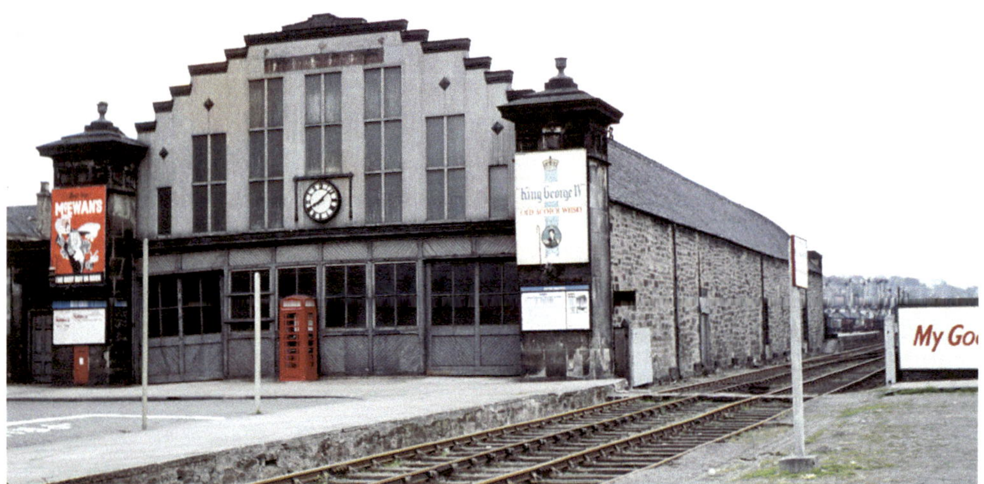

Dundee East Station

The third of Dundee's main stations, Dundee East, was located a short distance away from the other two at East Dock Street. It was originally built for the Dundee & Arbroath Railway Company in 1857, replacing an earlier one in nearby Trades Lane. Following nationalisation and line closures the station became surplus to requirements and it was closed on 5 January 1959. It was later demolished.

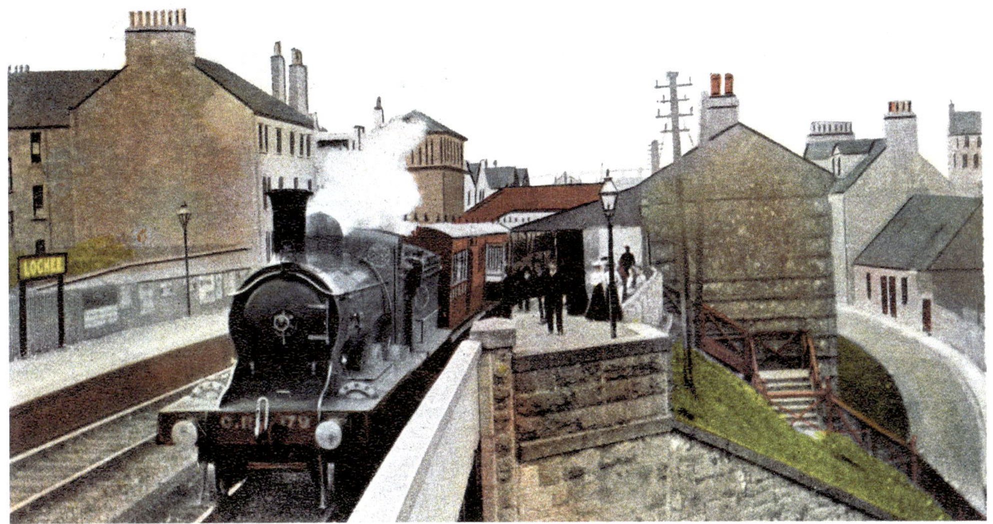

Lochee Station

The Dundee & Newtyle Railway opened in 1831. In 1861, the line took a diversion through Lochee. As well as Lochee Station, shown here, there were two other stations in the suburb – Lochee West (or Camperdown) and Liff, which, despite its name, was not located in the village of Liff but on South Road. The line closed to passengers in 1955 and the bridge was later demolished. The station building is now the Park Bar.

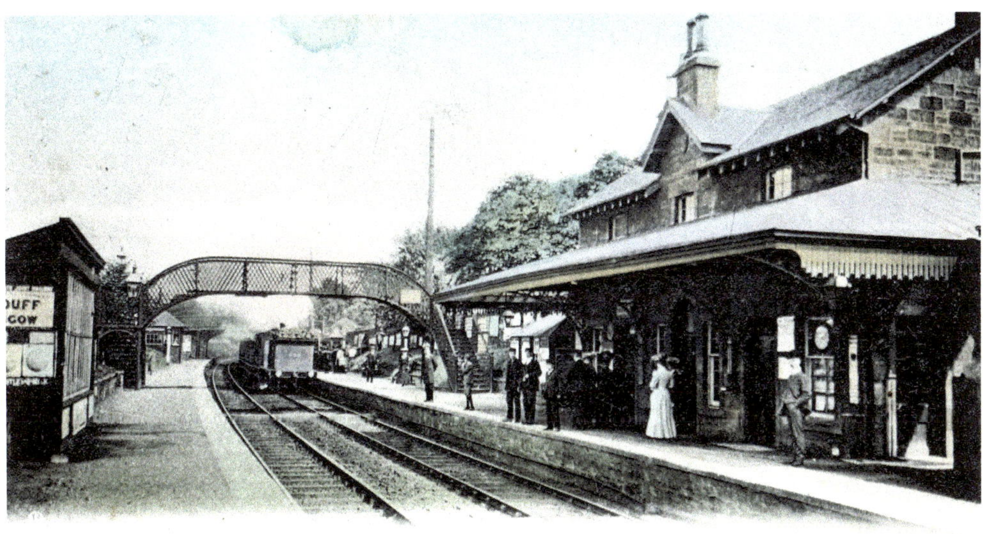

West Ferry Station

While Broughty Ferry Station survives as a working railway station, its near neighbours at Barnhill and West Ferry do not. In the case of West Ferry, however, the track and former station building remain today, making it easy to pinpoint the location today. The station was in operation for just over a century from the 1850s to the 1960s.

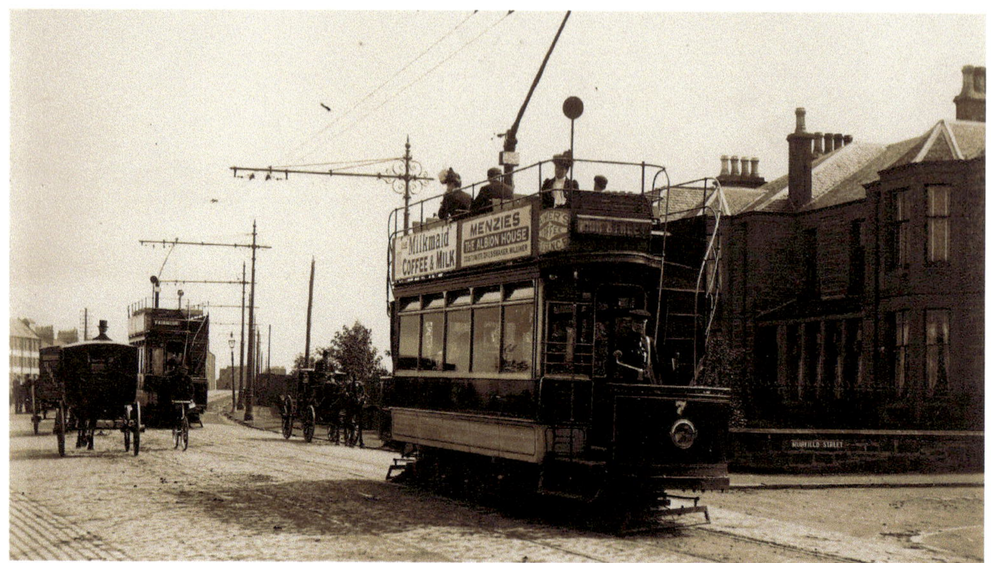

Trams

The first trams in Dundee were horse drawn, with the service beginning in 1877. These were later joined by steam trams in 1885 and finally by electric ones in 1900. Gradually, the electric trams took over. This early electric tram (car No. 7) is seen on Strathmartine Road near Fairmuir. The top decks of the trams were, as shown here, originally open to the elements but were later enclosed.

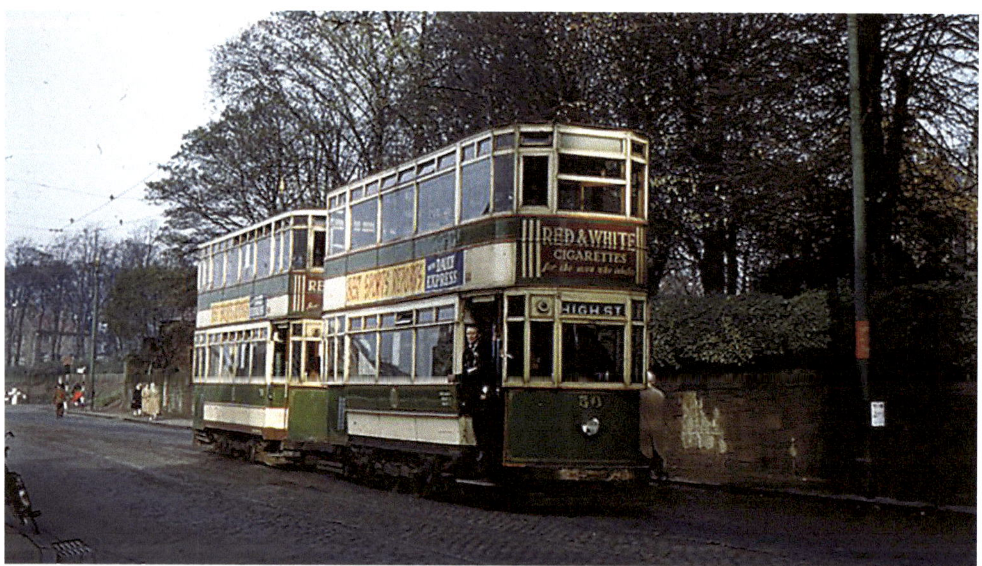

Lochee Tram Terminus

The Lochee tram terminus was situated on Coupar Angus Road near what is now Lochee Parish Church (previously known as Lochee West). Dundee's tram system closed on 20 October 1956, though some lines had been closed before this. The final tram was bound for Lochee making its way into the depot on the High Street rather than arriving at this terminus as there was, of course, no return journey to start.

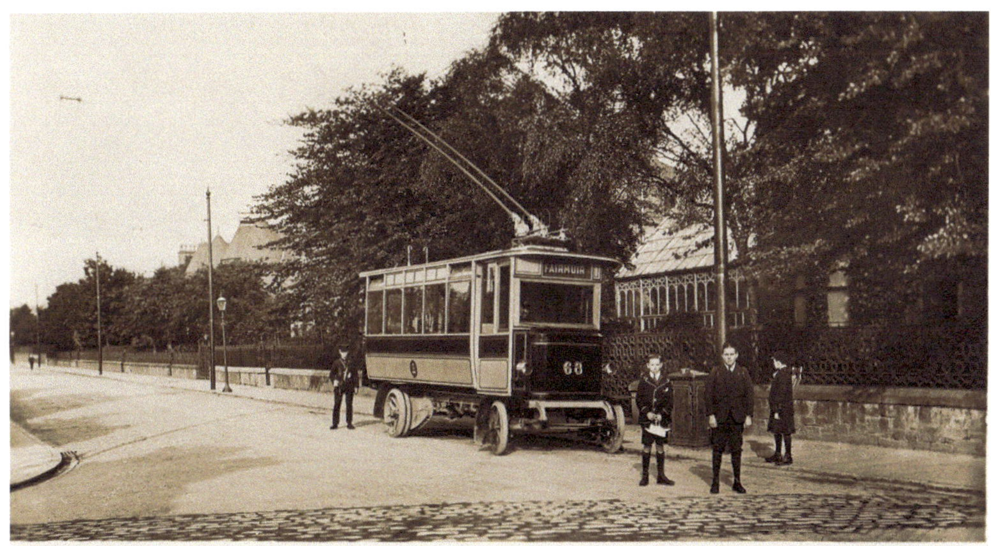

THE NEW TRACKLESS TROLLEY CAR, DUNDEE.

Trolleybuses

From 1912 Dundee operated a trolleybus service on a simple straight route along Clepington Road, between Forfar Road and Strathmartine Road with a turning circle at each end. Ultimately the trolleybuses were not successful. People complained about the bumpiness of the ride and the amount of dust generated. Plans to extend the service were abandoned and the service was withdrawn in1914. This picture shows one of the two vehicles that ran on the route at the Forfar Road end.

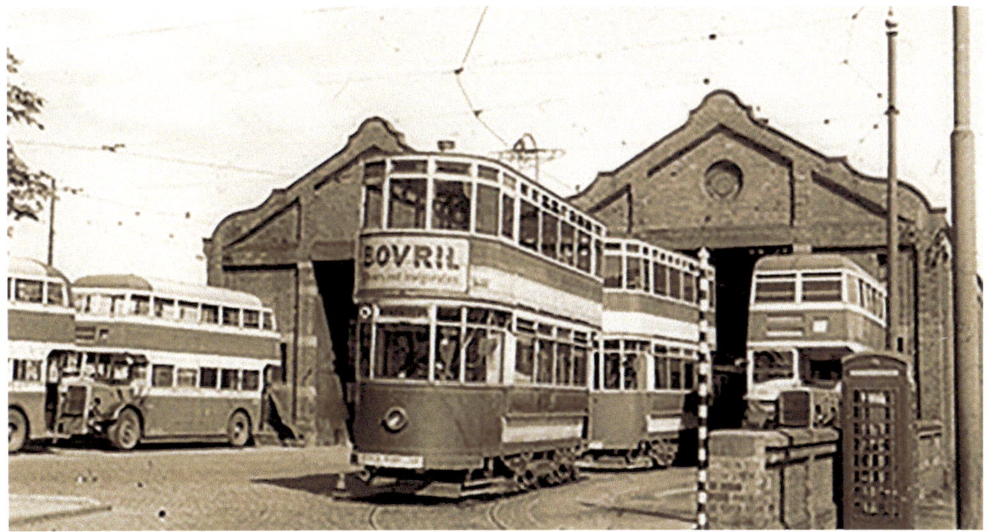

Maryfield Tram Depot

Maryfield tram depot dates from 1901 and was one of Dundee's main tram depots. It was extended twice and could hold up to seventy trams. Following the ending of the tram service in 1956 it was used as a garage for buses. After this, the depot fell into disrepair but was later earmarked as an appropriate permanent home for the Dundee Museum of Transport.

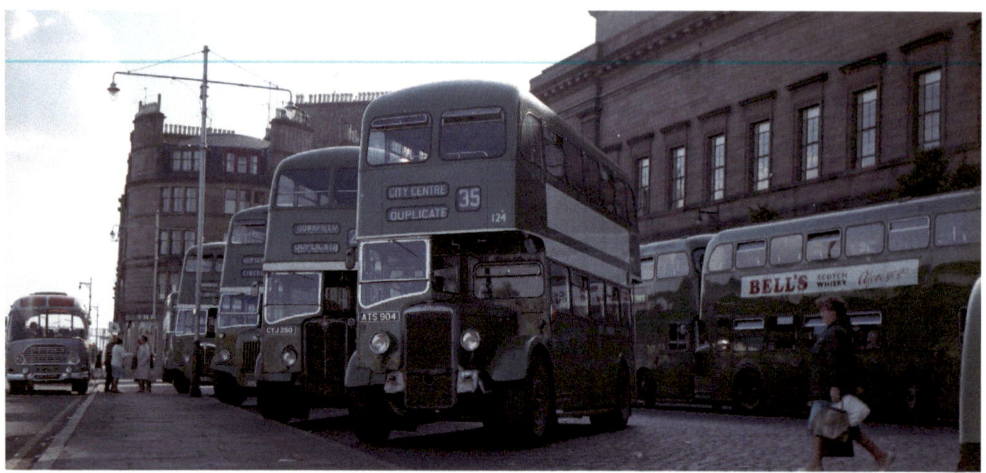

Shore Terrace

Corporation buses ran alongside trams in Dundee from 1921 when the first single-deck vehicles were introduced, with the first double-deckers appearing ten years later. Buses took over completely when the trams stopped running in 1956. This bus stance at Shore Terrace acted as acted as a hub and it was possible to travel to most places in the city from here. These buses were boarded by an open platform to the rear and would have had a conductor on board.

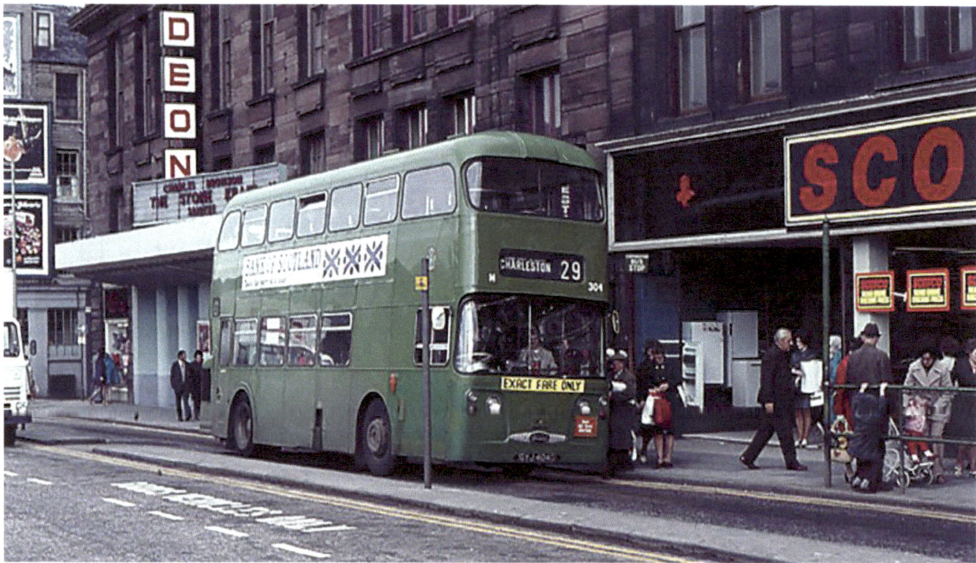

Exact Fare Buses

New technology in the 1970s meant that buses could be operated by a driver alone, without the need for a conductor. The fare would be put into a machine beside the driver's cab and a ticket would be issued. Buses, like this one in the Cowgate, carried a reminder that unlike the conductors, the machine would not give change. The film at the Odeon is the thriller *The Stone Killer* starring Charles Bronson, which dates the photograph to 1973.

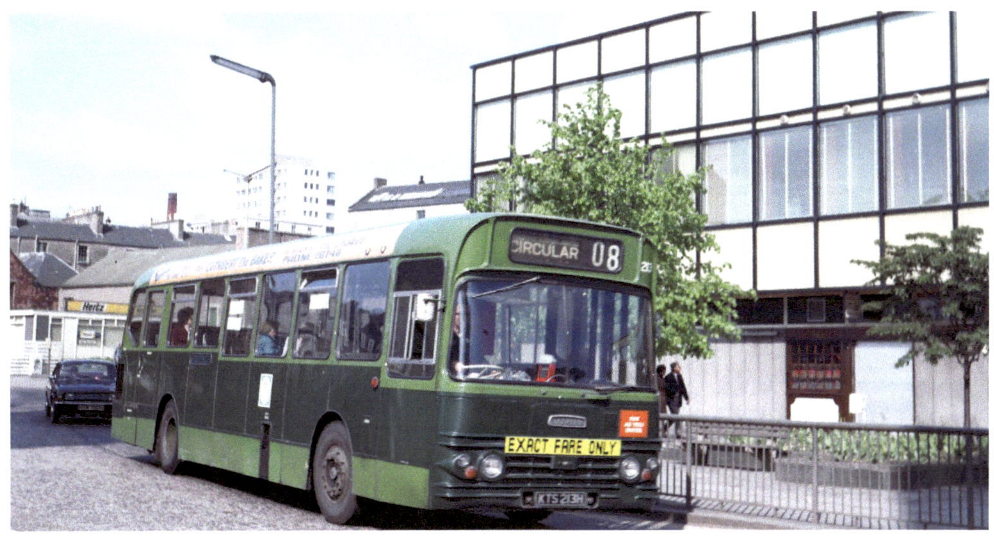

Single-deck Bus

A 1970s view of a single-deck exact fare bus passing the Angus Hotel on the Nethergate side. This type of Daimler bus had seating for forty-six people and had two sets of doors – one at the front for boarding and another in the middle for leaving the bus. A Tayside Regional Council sticker has been placed over the Dundee coat of arms on the side of the bus, meaning the image dates from after local government reorganisation in 1975.

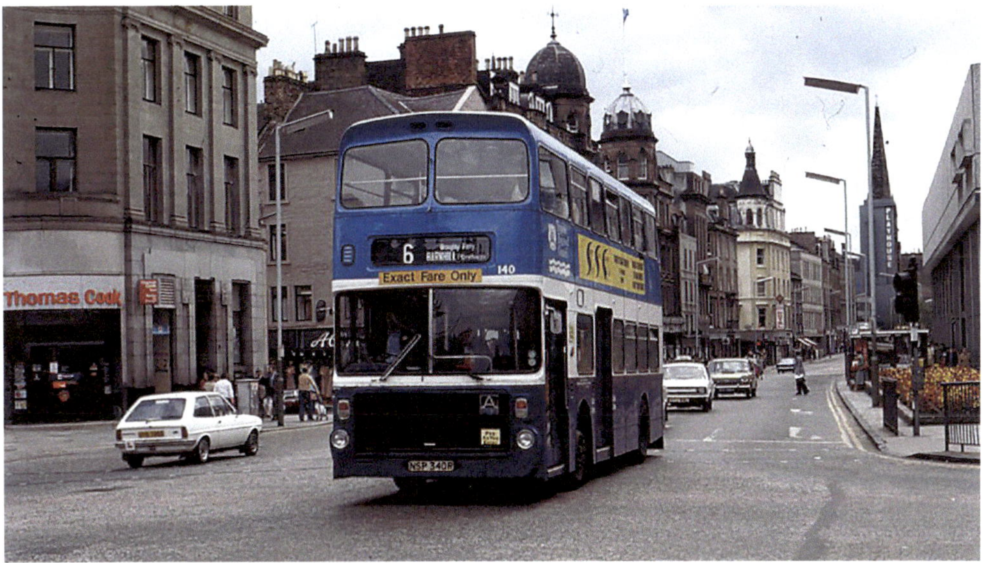

Tayside Regional Council Bus

Following the reorganisation of local government, the responsibility for Dundee's buses passed to the new Tayside Regional Council. This meant that the city's green buses were repainted in the blue livery of the new regional authority. Visible in the distance here is the tower of Green's Playhouse as it appeared at the time – encased in grey ribbed metal.

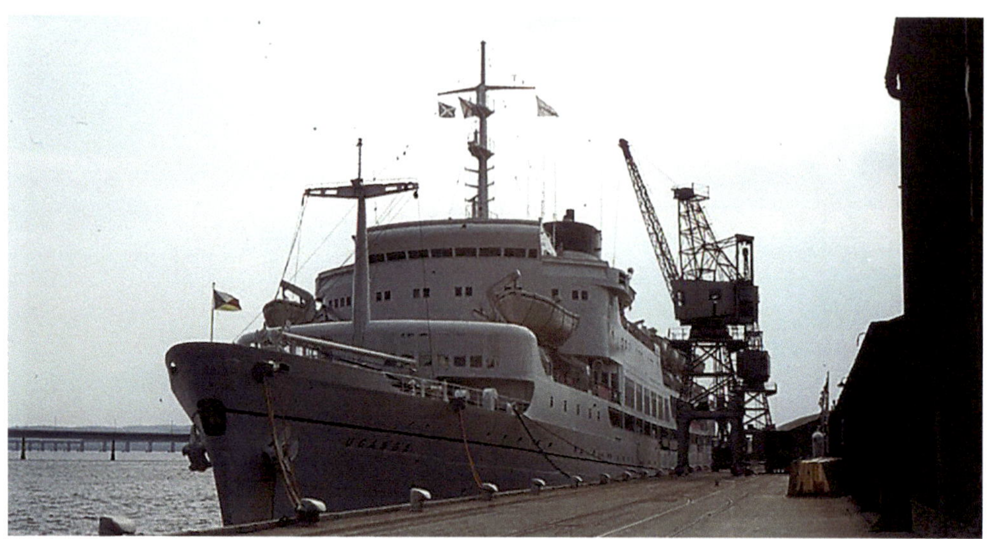

SS *Uganda*

SS *Uganda* is seen here at Dundee docks. The steamship was launched as a passenger liner in 1952 but is perhaps best remembered as an educational cruise ship, a role it took on in 1968. Many in Dundee will remember going on school cruises aboard the *Uganda*. In 1982 the ship took on another role as a hospital ship in the Falklands conflict. The *Uganda* was laid up in 1985 and ultimately scrapped in 1992.

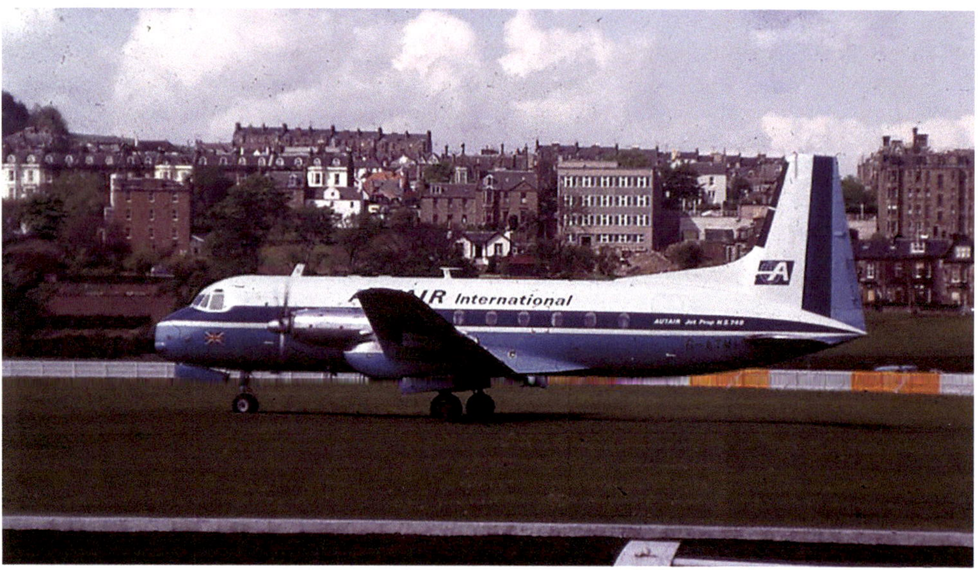

Dundee Airport

Dundee Airport opened at Riverside in 1963 on land reclaimed from the River Tay. This photograph shows a plane at the airport in the 1960s when the runway was grass, rather than tarmac. There have been scheduled flights to various destinations over the years. There are currently flights to London and Shetland. The view uphill to the Perth Road area is now largely obscured by trees.

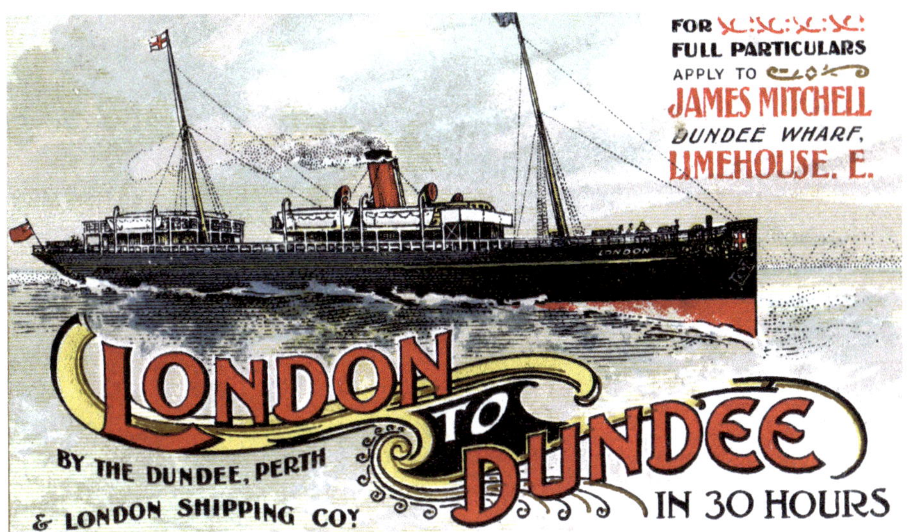

Dundee, Perth & London Shipping Co. Ltd

The Dundee, Perth & London Shipping Company was created in July 1826 from the merger of two older companies – the Dundee & Perth Shipping Company (founded in 1798) and the Dundee & Perth Union Shipping Company (founded in 1819). As seen in this old advertisement, the company offered cargo and passenger services between Dundee and London. Steamships were introduced on this line in 1834. Though no longer involved in shipping, the company survives today as the DP & L Group.

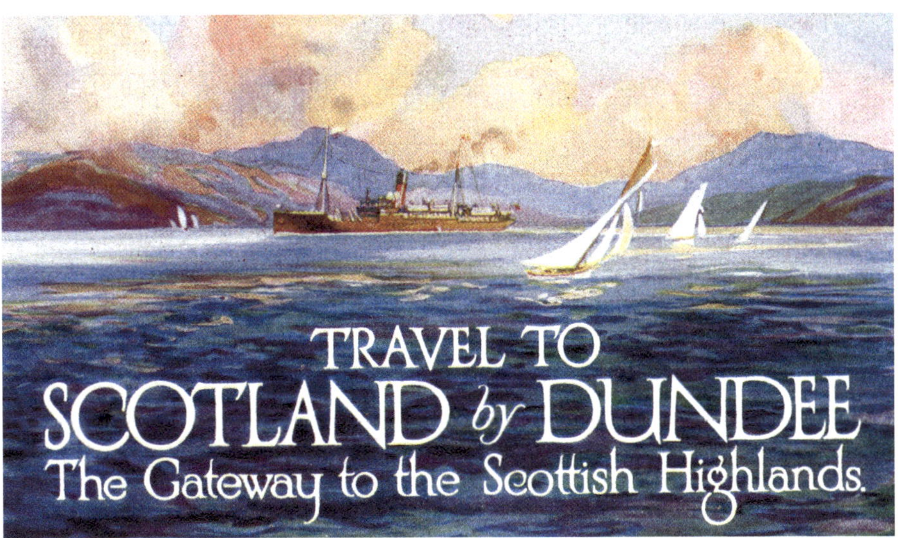

Dundee: The Gateway to the Scottish Highlands

Dundee today is certainly more of a tourist destination in itself than was the case when this 1920s DPL illustration advertising the city as the Gateway to the Scottish Highlands was published, though it does remain a good base from which to explore much of Scotland. The voyage on the SS *Perth* from London to Dundee and back could be combined with further trips to destinations including Crieff, Perth, St Andrews and Braemar.

6

Disappearing Dundee

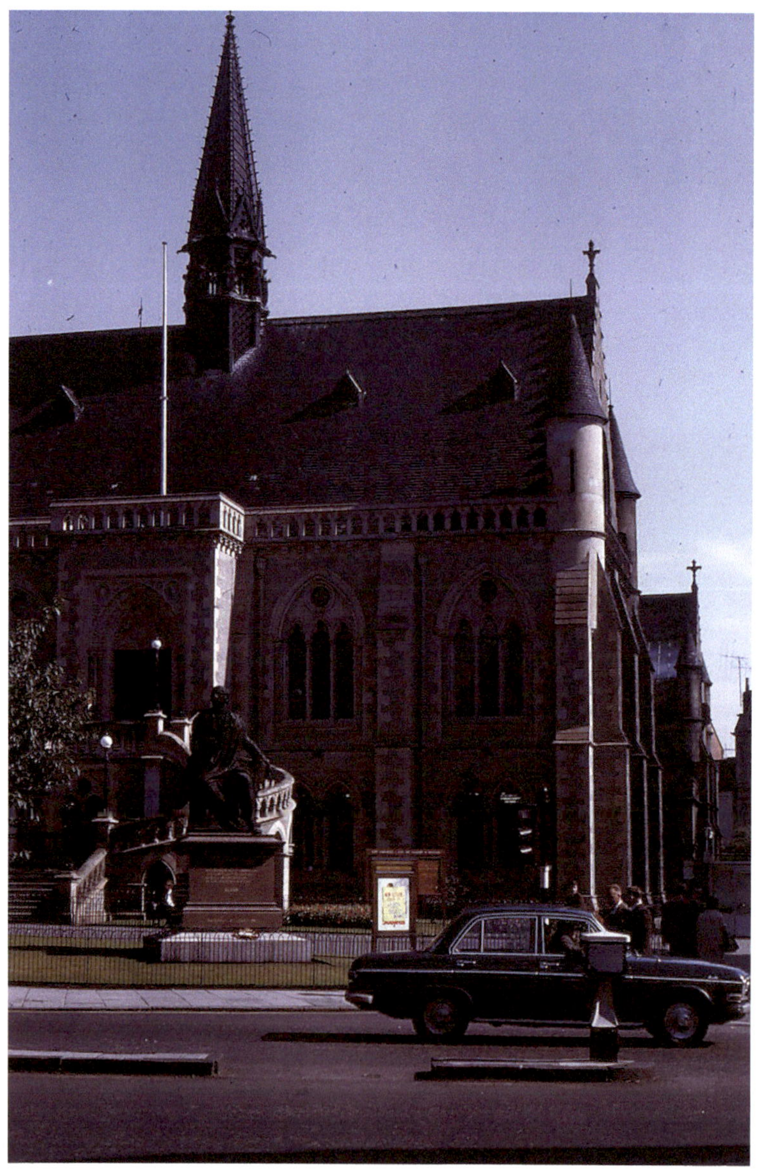

A 1960s view of the Albert institute and Robert Burns statue.

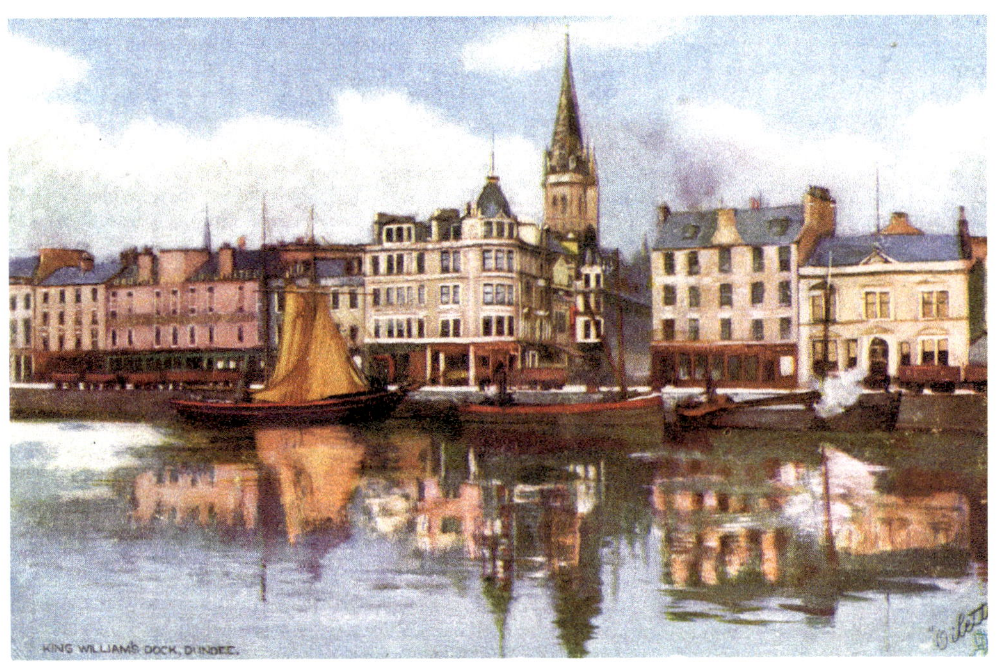

King William IV Dock

The King William IV Dock opened in 1834 and takes its name from the then current monarch. As we have seen, it was filled in in the 1960s. Its former location can be deduced from the position of the building on the left-hand corner of the junction of Dock Street and Commercial Street, which still survives today, and also from the spire of St Paul's Episcopal Cathedral.

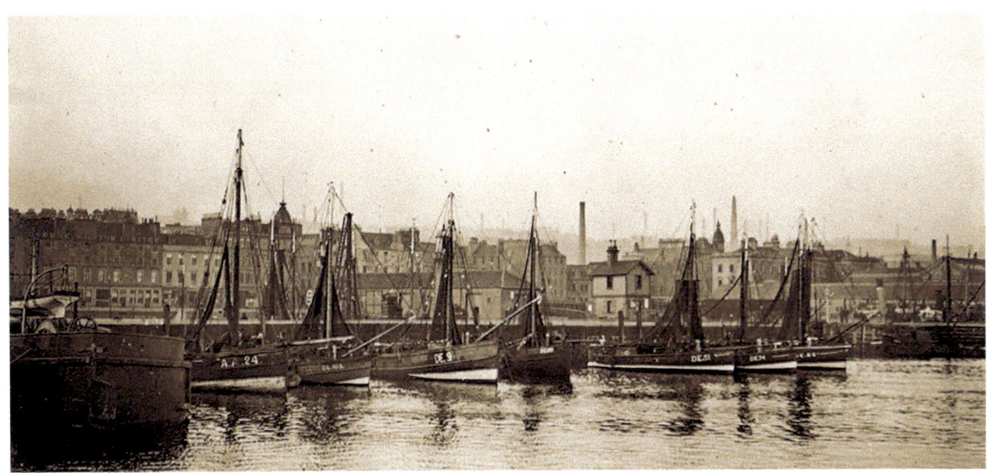

Tidal Harbour

The Tidal Harbour was situated in front of the William IV Dock. This view looks across towards Dock Street where the premises of George Morton Limited, famous for their OVD rum, is visible on the left of this picture. The fishing boats here all have the DE code, which represents Dundee, except for the one on the left, which bears the AA of Alloa.

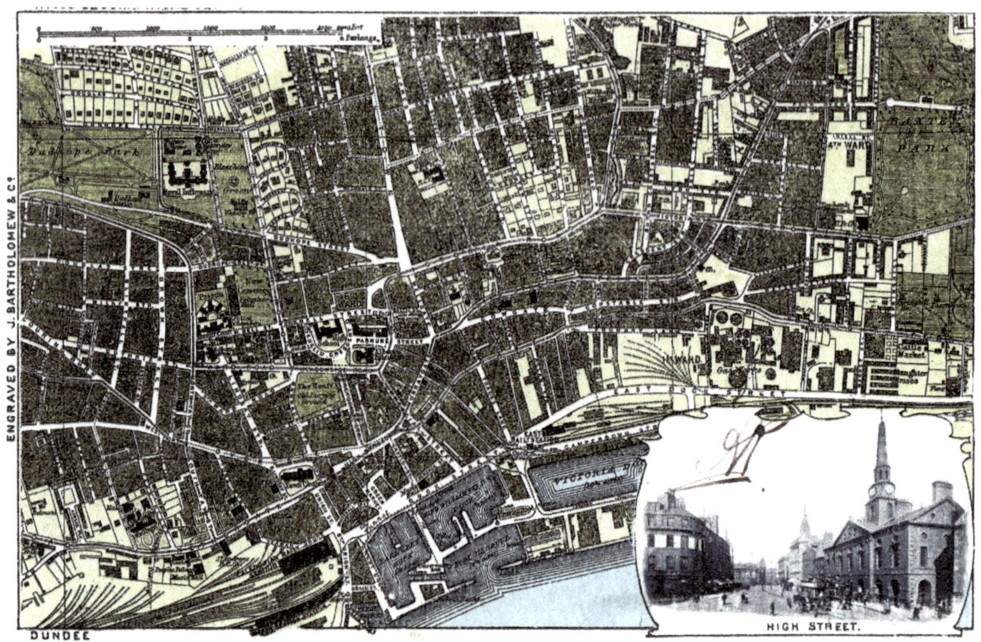

Map Showing Docks

This old postcard map dating from the early twentieth century is useful for showing the location of many of the lost streets that feature in the pages of this book. It also shows the position of the Earl Grey and King William IV docks, which were filled in to make way for the construction of the Tay Road Bridge in the 1960s.

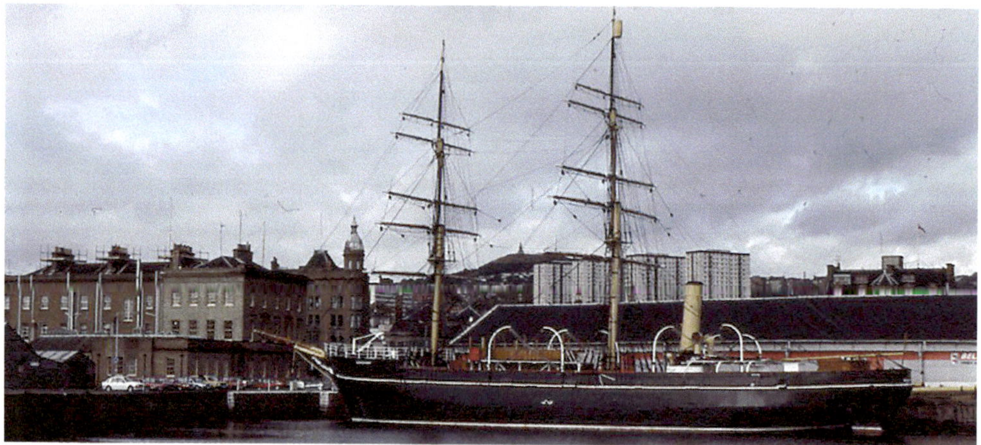

RRS *Discovery*

RRS (Royal Research Ship) *Discovery* was built in Dundee, launched in 1901 and is said to be the last traditional wooden three-masted ship to be built in the United Kingdom. The *Discovery* took Robert Falcon Scott and Ernest Shackleton on their first journey to the Antarctic with the British National Antarctic Expedition. In 1986, *Discovery* returned to Dundee and was, as seen here, berthed at Victoria Dock, until a custom-built dock and visitor centre, Discovery Point, was opened in 1992.

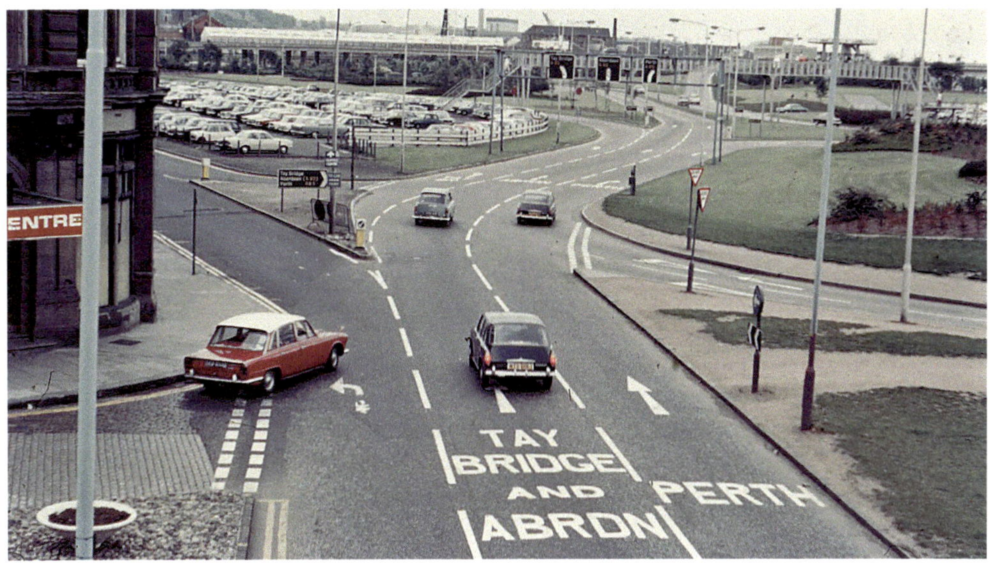

Tay Bridge Approaches

Following the removal of the docks and the construction of the Tay Road Bridge, the area between the city centre and the River Tay was redeveloped with motor traffic very much in mind, with the area becoming a patchwork of roads and traffic islands. Pedestrians were supposed to be restricted to the overhead walkways but the well-worn pathway on the right of the picture shows this was not always followed.

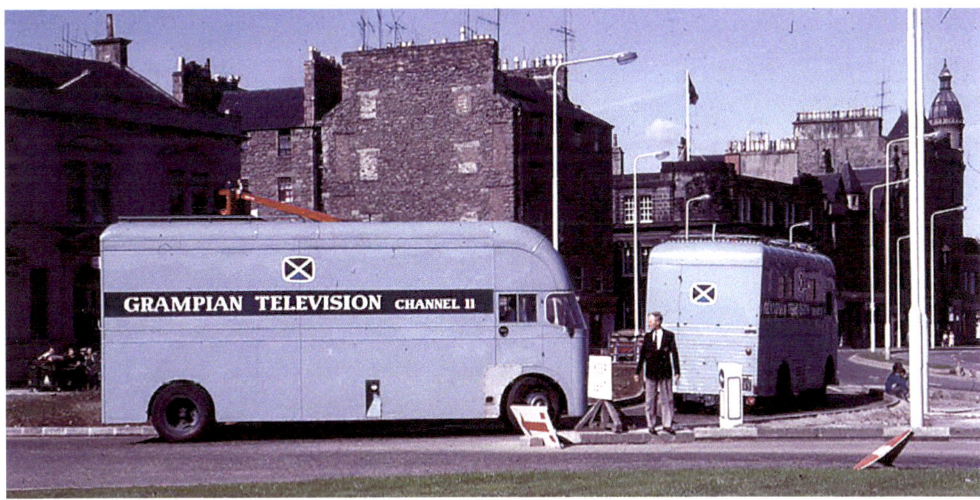

Grampian TV Vans at Dock Street

This image shows a part of Dock Street in August 1966. The buildings to the left have long gone but those after the opening of Gellatly Street remain. The Grampian Television vans are there to cover the opening of the Tay Road Bridge. Grampian is described as Channel II, because until BBC2 Scotland launched the previous month, people in the region would only have had two TV channels: one BBC channel and Grampian as the local ITV region.

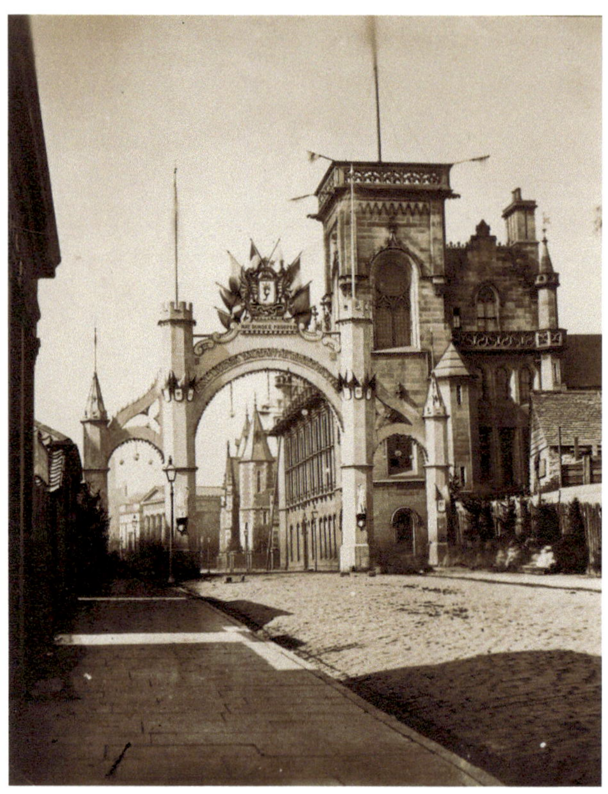

Triumphal Arch, Panmure Street

The opening of Baxter Park was marked by a 2-mile-long procession from Barrack Park to the new park. Along the route several triumphal arches were erected including this one at Panmure Street designed by painter A. W. Fairweather and built by joiner William Young. The arch was mainly paid for by Cowgate merchants. At the top of the structure, it says 'May Dundee prosper' and around the arch it says 'Long live Sir David and the Misses Baxter'.

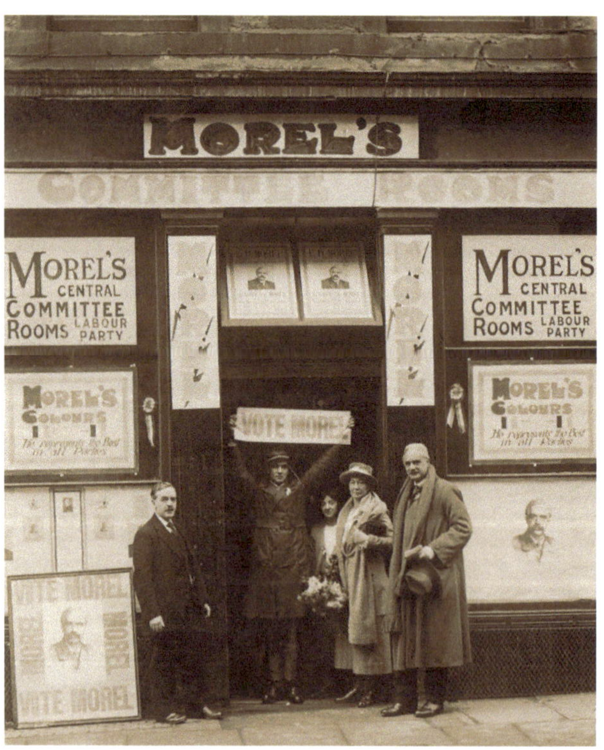

E. D. Morel

It is well known that Winston Churchill was MP for Dundee and that he was defeated by Edwin Scrymgeour, who, to date, is the only prohibitionist elected to Parliament. This telling of the story neglects to mention, however, that Dundee was at that time a two-member constituency and that the Labour candidate, the French-born campaigning journalist, author and pacifist E. D. Morel, also defeated Churchill. Morrel is seen here at his campaign headquarters in Panmure Street.

William McGonagall

William McGonagall, often cited as the world's worst poet, is forever associated with Dundee where he spent most of his life, though he was born and died in Edinburgh. He began writing poetry in 1877 and eventually wrote around 200 poems, including 'The Tay Bridge Disaster'. The derision and ridicule with which he was greeted by Dundee audiences was matched only by his own oblivious self-confidence. Nevertheless, McGonagall is still published and discussed today while more talented poets are forgotten.

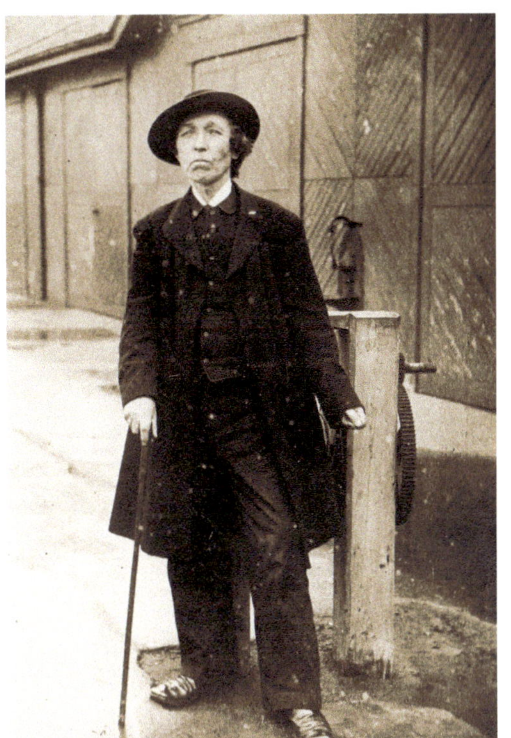

Blind Hughie

Hugh Lennox – 'Blind Hughie' – would have been as well known on the streets of Dundee in the late nineteenth century as William McGonagall. A native of Lauder, he lost his sight as a child and spent much of his life as a street singer. He was said to have a sweet voice and a fondness for Scottish songs. He died in Dundee in 1887 at the age of sixty-two.

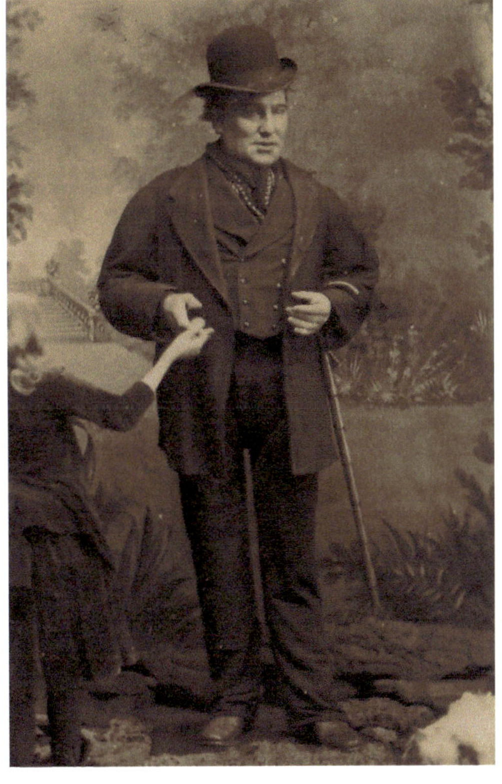

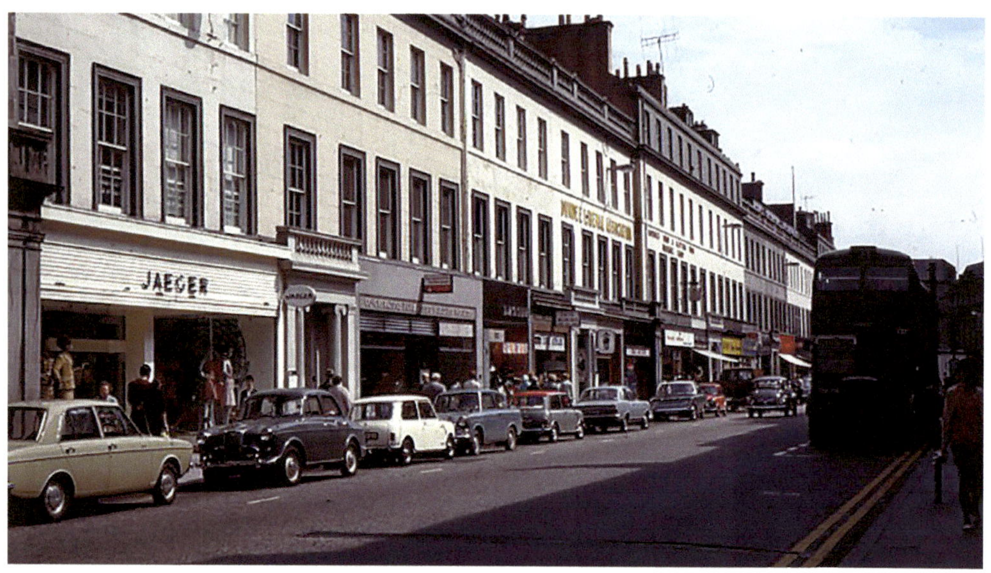

Reform Street

Reform Street is little changed from this 1960s view in that all the buildings survive but the appearance and atmosphere of the street are much changed over the years. Perhaps most notably, traffic was allowed in the 1960s but the today the street is pedestrianised. Sadly, changes in shopping habits have meant that the number of occupied shops has declined in recent years too.

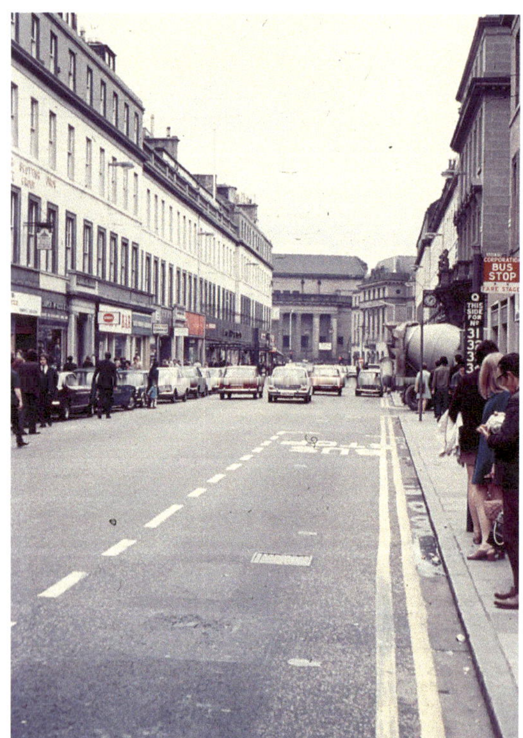

Wimpy, Reform Street

Another view of Reform Street, this time in the 1970s. Many will remember the Wimpy Bar, which opened in the 1960s and was one of the first places you could buy an American-style hamburger in Dundee, albeit served on a real plate with metal cutlery. The Wimpy lasted until 1987 when it moved to new premises in the Murraygate. Reform Street, meanwhile, became home to Scotland's first branch of McDonald's that same year.

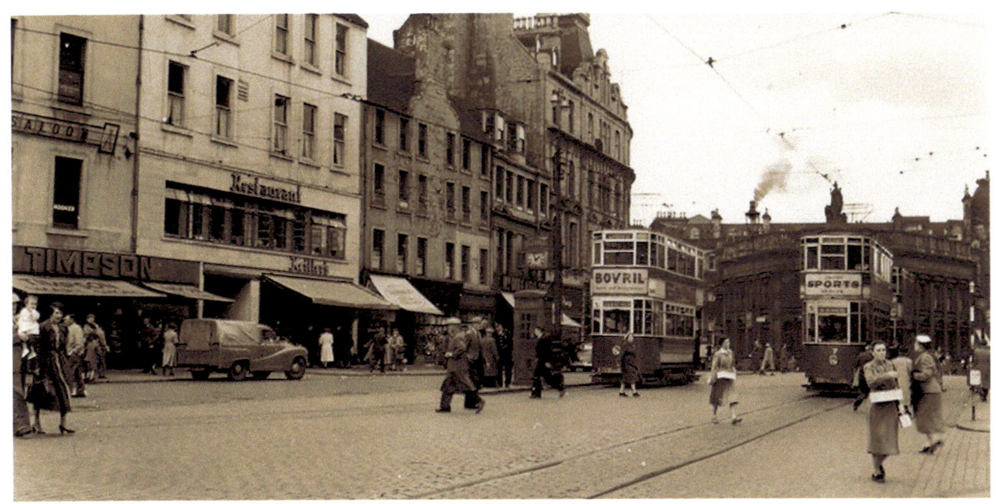

High Street

The most noticeable difference between the High Street in the early 1950s when this photograph was taken and today is the presence of trams. As can be seen, though, motor traffic was also able to access the area. This increased greatly over the decades that followed. Today, however, the entire area between Commercial Street and Crichton Street has been given over to pedestrians.

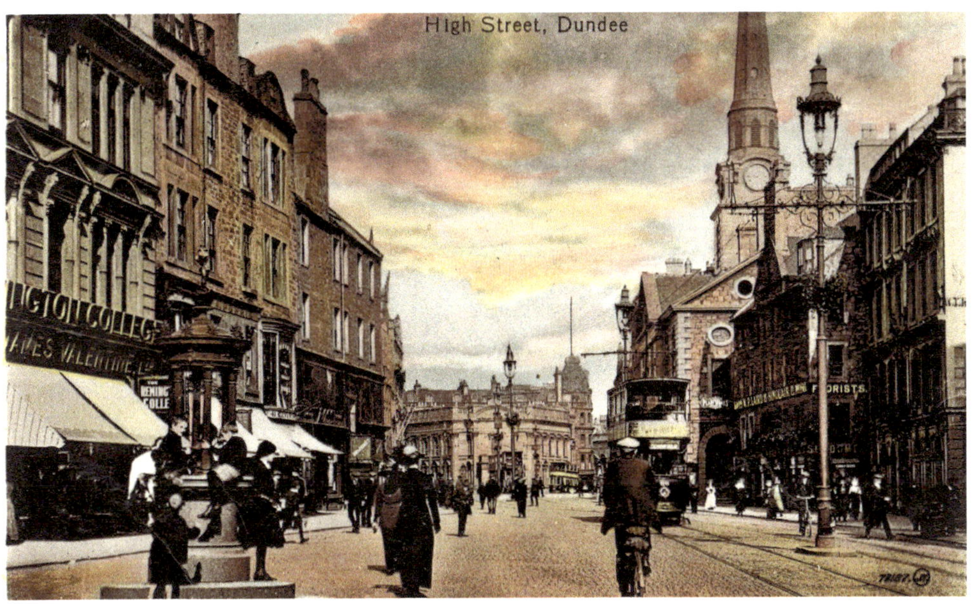

Caird Fountain

On the left-hand side of this image is the Caird Fountain, which was donated to the city by textile manufacturer Edward Caird, father of Sir James Key Caird, who donated Caird Hall and Caird Park. Caird suggested a fountain in 1861 but it was not until 1879 that it was erected. It soon became a familiar landmark. The fountain was not well maintained and fell into disrepair. It was removed to Caird Park in 1927. Today only its base survives.

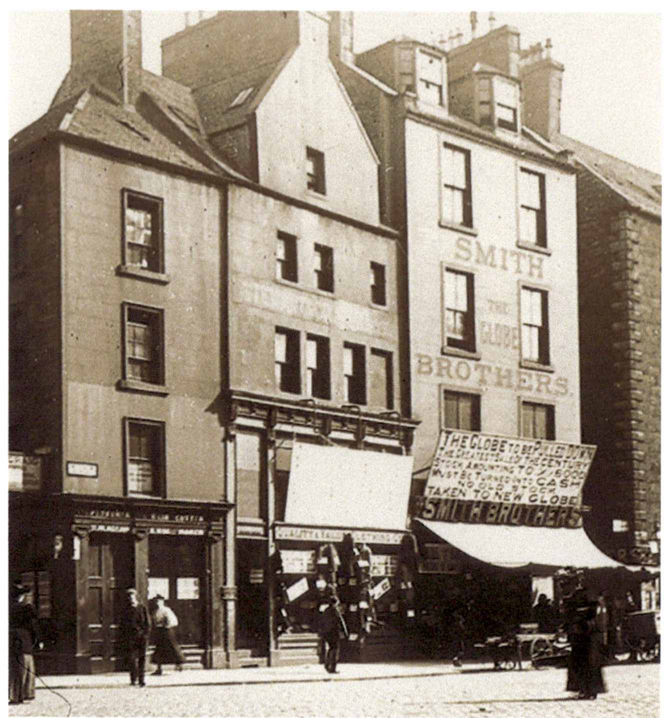

Smith Brothers at the Globe

Smith Brothers began as a small clothier's shop in Reform Street in 1884 before moving to this three-storey building, known as the Globe, at the High Street near its junction with Castle Street in 1890. Six years later they were given notice to quit because the building, as the sign in this photograph states, was 'to be pulled down'. The company relocated to new premises in the Murraygate.

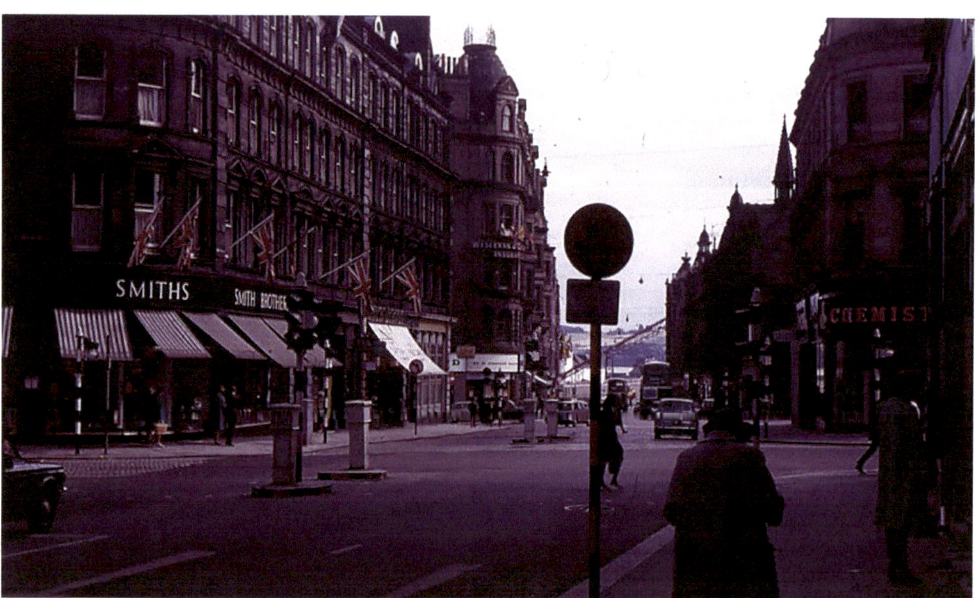

Smith Brothers at Murraygate

Smith Brothers' Murraygate premises is shown here in the 1960s. As well as the original clothing business, the business expanded into home furnishing. Following the closure of Smith Brothers in 1970, the building was taken over by their then parent company Grants, an Edinburgh furniture company. The shop was later home to John Menzies and the section shown here is now the Body Shop.

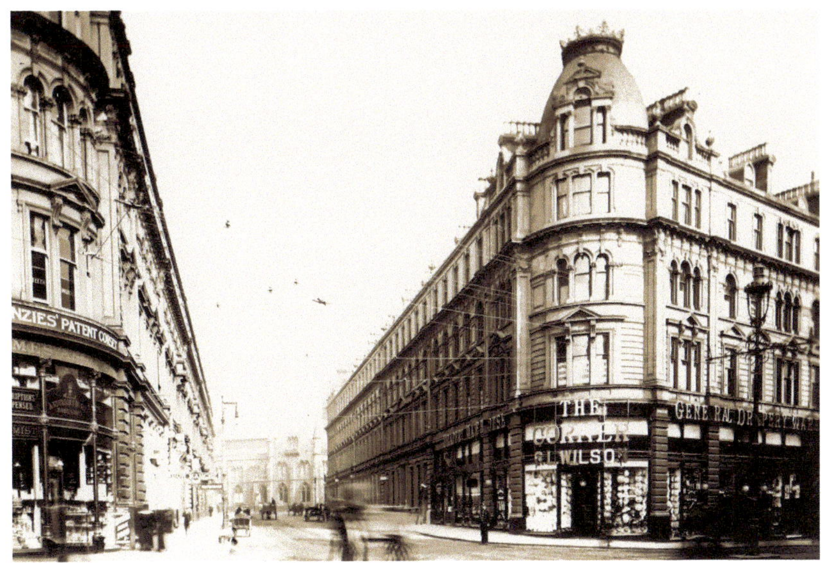

G. L. Wilson's

The junction of Murraygate and Commercial Street was at one time the site of three of Dundee's most famous departments stores – Smith Brothers, D. M. Brown's and G. L. Wilson's. Wilson's store was known as 'The Corner'. The building was acquired by draper Gavin Laurie Wilson in 1894. Wilson's sons Garnet and John later became involved in the family business. Garnet Wilson went on to be Lord Provost of Dundee from 1940 to 1946. The department store closed in December 1971.

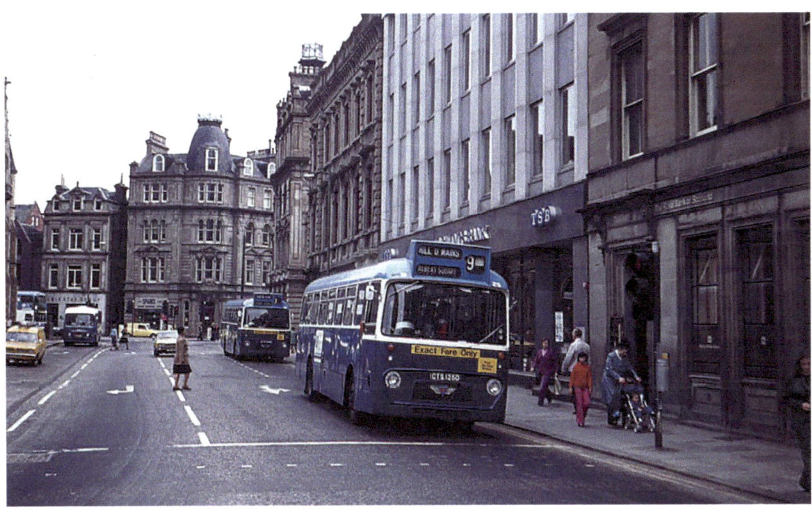

Meadowside

This section of road might be confusing for some as it has two street signs, one saying Meadowside and the other Albert Square. This is because Albert Square is the larger square of which Meadowside forms a part. It is not likely to be a problem for drivers, though, as the area has long since been pedestrianised. The TSB branch visible in this picture remains today but the neighbouring Royal Bank, like several former banks in the city, is now a pub.

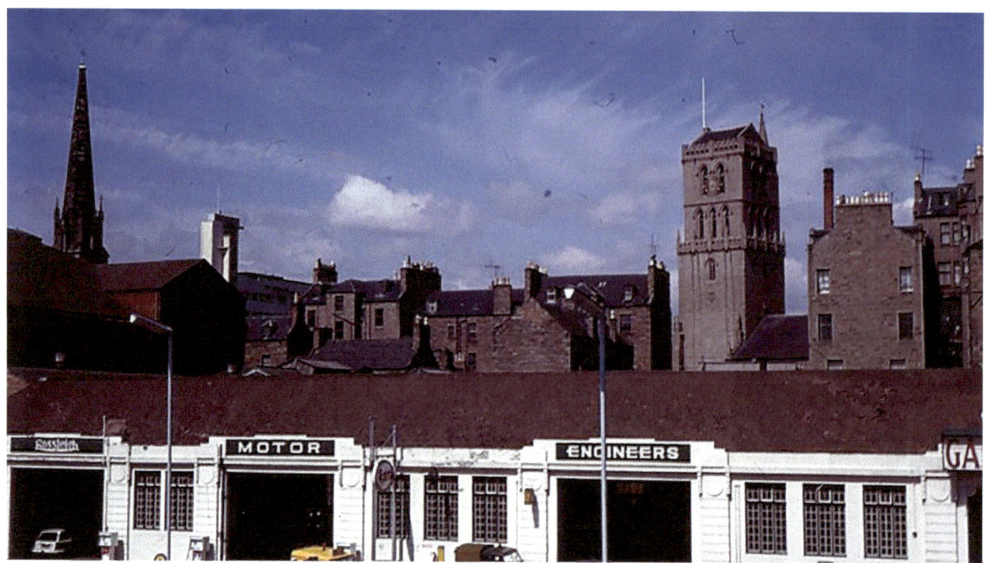

Yeaman Shore

Yeaman Shore is believed to have taken the first part of its name from the Yeaman family of Dryburgh, near Lochee. The 'shore' part comes from the fact that this area once marked the edge of the water. This late 1960s view is dominated by the Rossleigh Garage. Whitehall House, home of Thorntons solicitors, occupies this site today, though the height of that building means that the view over to the Nethergate and beyond has gone.

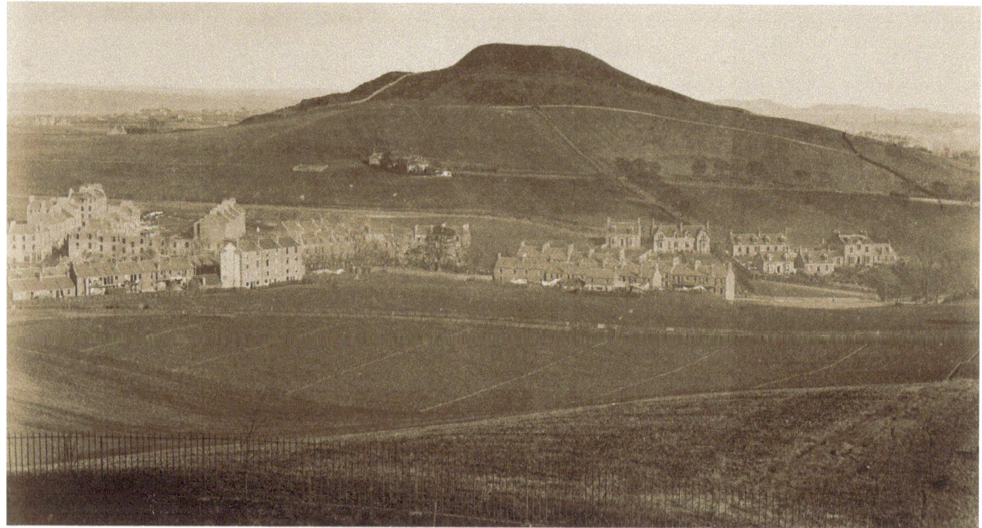

Dundee Law

Dundee Law is the result of volcanic activity around 400 million years ago and during the Iron Age was the site of a hill fort. This nineteenth-century image of the Law looks particularly bare to modern eyes as it is without the war memorial, road to the summit, communications mast or trees that have since been added. The lower slopes of the Law have also been much built upon in the intervening years.

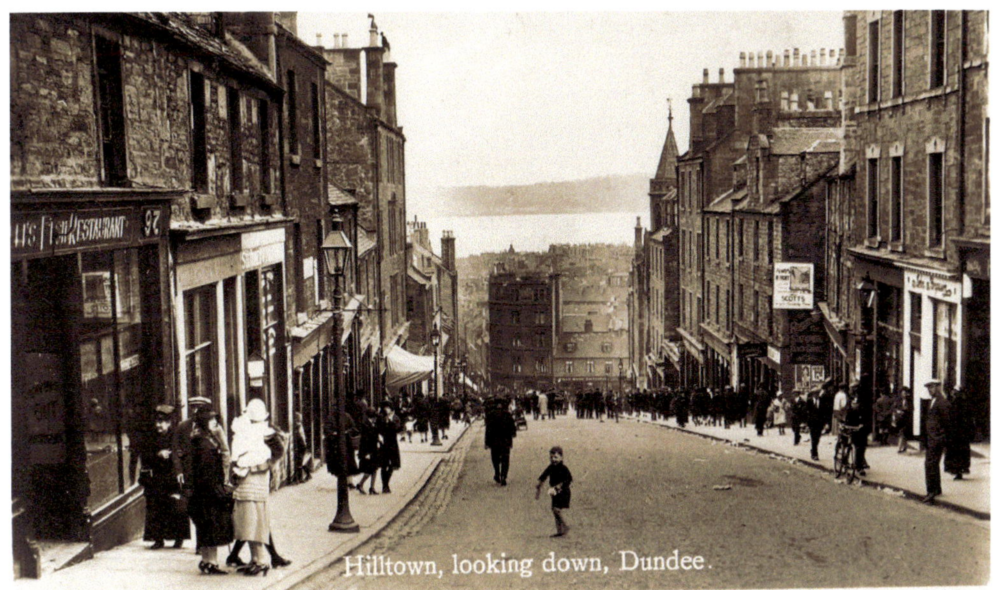

Hilltown

The Hilltown was once a separate barony outside the Burgh of Dundee. It was also known Rottenrow or the Bonnethill, the latter because it was mainly inhabited by bonnet makers, one of the Nine Incorporated Trades of Dundee. This early twentieth-century view shows that the Hilltown was still a thriving area at this time, as can be seen in the number of people heading to and from the city centre.

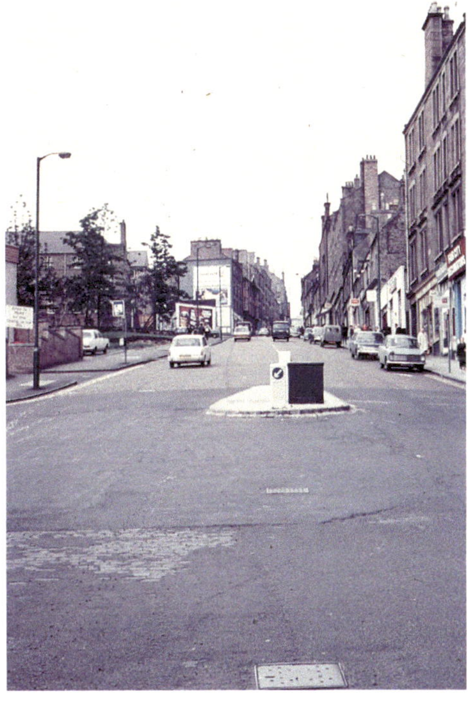

Hilltown, 1960s

A 1960s image of the Hilltown in the opposite direction from the previous view. By this time the area was changing, with multistorey blocks of flats at the top and bottom of the hill joining the more traditional tenements. Cars were common too, though this section of the Hilltown was always considered too steep for buses and trams, which never operated there.

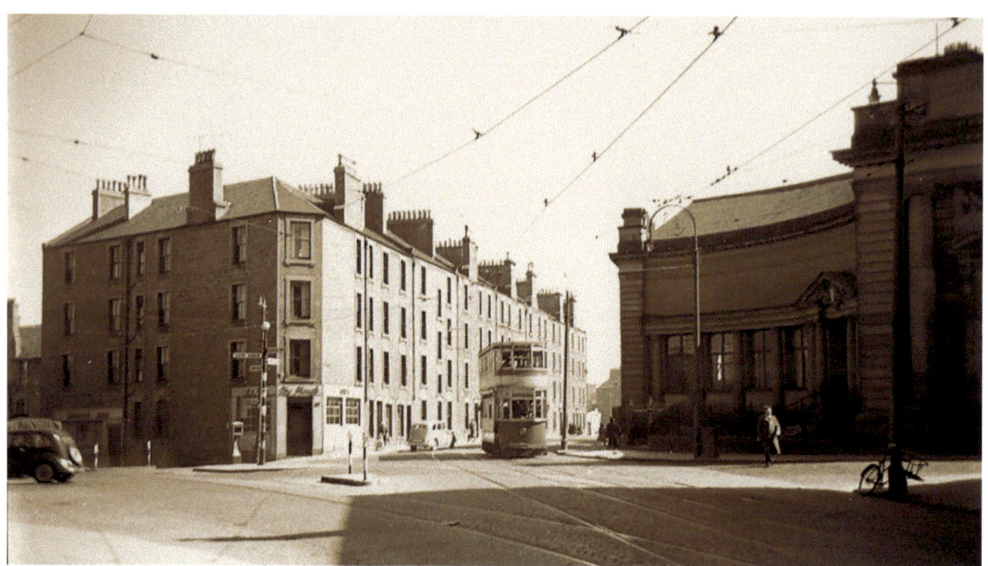

Coldside

This 1950s view of Coldside is still recognisable today, but there are a few important differences. Most notably, in this view there is no traffic roundabout – or circle as it is known in Dundee. The roundabout's introduction was particularly helpful in easing the flow of traffic at this well-known five-way junction. The pub here is called The Plough. It was renamed Frew's when publican Willie Frew moved his business there from the Hawkhill.

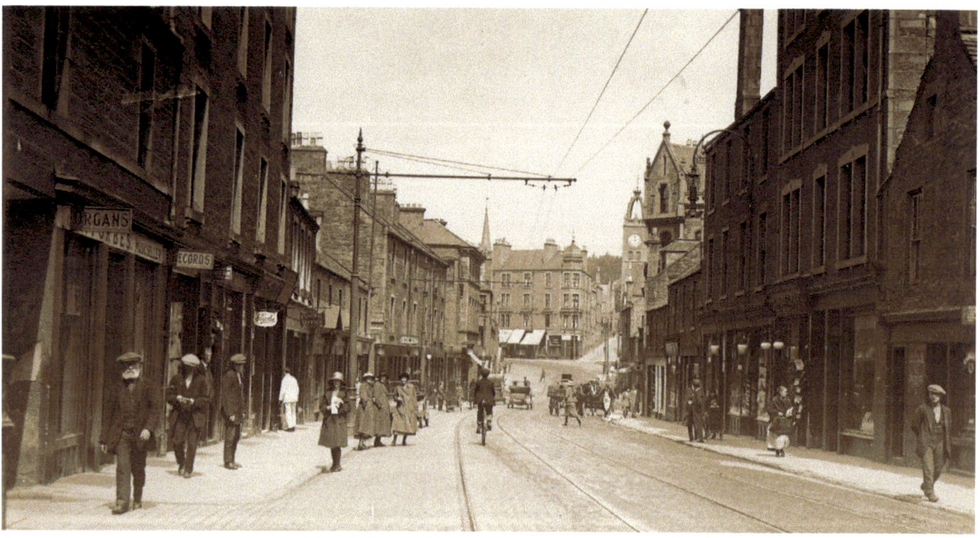

Lochee High Street

Lochee was originally a separate village but became part of Dundee in 1859. Lochee High Street is shown here around a century ago. All the buildings on the left-hand side of this view have been demolished, as have some of the buildings that replaced them. Most of the right-hand side survives with the notable exception of Lochee East Church, which was demolished in 1960.

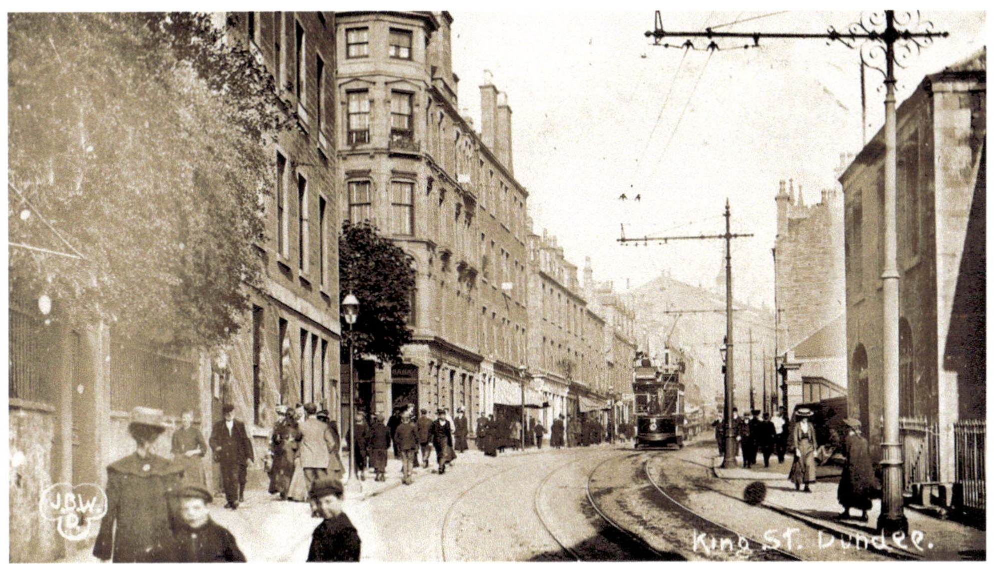

King Street

You will still find King Street on a map of Dundee but, like many once bustling neighbourhoods on the fringes of the city centre, it is much quieter in terms of pedestrian traffic than it appears in this early twentieth-century view. Most of the buildings have gone too. The most notable survivor is the Baxter's mill building in the distance.

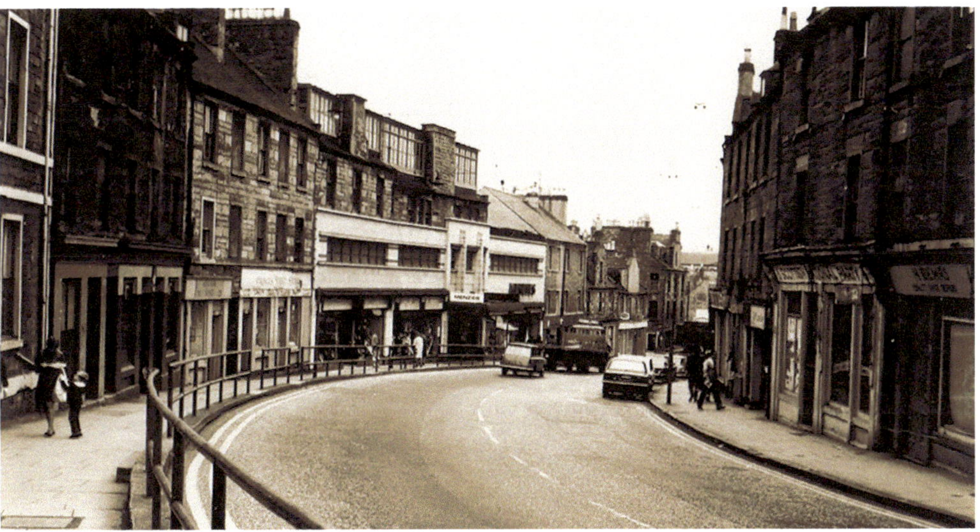

Princes Street

If little survives of King Street as it once was, then nearby Princes Street has undergone an even bigger transformation. This picture was taken in the 1970s and not one of the buildings shown here is still standing. Prominent among them is the Menzies and Sons Limited store at Nos 93–117. The family-run business, which sold clothes and household goods, started in a small shop on this site in the early twentieth century.

Acknowledgements

Most of the images are from my own collection or were taken by me, except for the following

Page 29 National Tramway Museum Photographic Collection
Pages 26 (lower), 27 (top), 35 (top), 36, and 39 top Libraries, Leisure and Culture Dundee
Page 74 (lower) Ernie's Railway Archive
Page 87 (lower) National Archives

Every attempt has been made to seek permission for copyright material used in this book. However, if I have inadvertently used copyright material without permission/acknowledgement I apologise and will make the necessary correction at the first opportunity.

Select Bibliography

Archibald, Malcolm, *Dundee at a Glance* (Fort Publishing Limited, 2016)
Cronshaw, Andrew, *Old Dundee Picture Postcards* (Mainstream Publishing, 1988)
Dorward, David, *Dundee Names, Places and People* (Mercat Press, 1998)
Eunson, Eric, and Early, Bill, *Old Dundee* (Stenlake Publishing, 2002)
Gifford, John, *The Buildings of Scotland: Dundee and Angus* (Yale University Press, 2012)
McKean, Charles, and Walker, David, *Dundee: An Illustrated Introduction* (Royal Corporation of Architects/Scottish Academic Press, 1984)
McKean, Charles, Whatley, Patricia, and Baxter, Kenneth, *Lost Dundee* (Birlinn, 2008)